SO-BFE-356

'John Huffman has written a book that tells us marriage matters to God and therefore marriage should matter to us! He speaks from the scriptures - the Bible after all is an excellent book on the subject. With wisdom and winsomeness John has give us a book that can strengthen families and grow trust and love. I heartily recommend this book.'

Jill Briscoe

'Dr Huffman's book, entitled The Family You Want, is a biblically and faith-based, pragmatic resource for families and for those of us who work with families. Clearly it is a book which is helpful for an intergenerational manner to families.

Dr Huffman's sharing about himself and his own family and the reality of the challenges of Christian family living are very helpful in providing steps for improvement and hope. It is realistic and honest, and provides a healthy map for daily living.

Ralph H. Earle
Former President of American Association
of Marriage and Family Counsellors

'God has ordained three and only three institutions; the Church, government and the family. In this most significant book Pastor John Huffman has carefully and clearly addressed the needs and opportunities of both the nuclear family and the extended family. It is eminently practical, warmly relational and scripturally based.

Some months ago when I read some of Pastor Huffman's messages to his Church on the family, I strongly urged him to put these in manuscript form for a book. This you now hold in your hand. Even after 60+ years of marriage to the same wonderful lady, I found it most helpful to me as a concerned Christian. Don't take lightly what Pastor Huffman has to say in these pages. Responding to his insights will make for all of us family relationships that are even more meaningful.

The chapters on "How to Keep Your Family Emotionally Healthy", "What a Godly Parent Looks Like" and "When the Honeymoon Ends, the Marriage Can Begin" are worth the price of the book.

Ted Engstrom, President Emeritus, World Vision

'Of the making ... and breaking ... of families there is no end. And also of the writing of books about families there seems to be no end! But THE FAMILY YOU WANT should also be A BOOK YOU WANT TO READ! I highly recommend it, for our family relationships can be the cause both of the highest earthly joy, and also the deepest pain. My friend John Huffman has written a book that is both biblical and practical, with high ideals but a realistic understanding that we all struggle with this most important of human relations. His approach is thoughtful, his style clear. I know this book is authentic, because my wife and I know John and his wife Anne well. We have walked with them, as they have with us, the journeys of our marriages across the years ...the joys of love, the tragedy of losing an adult child, the challenges of matching two professional careers, the changes that decades bring. Through all of this John has been a faithful, devoted husband, father, pastor, and counsellor and friend to many. His words in this book are matched by the model of his own life. John would be the first to admit his own shortcomings, but also the first to aspire to a God-blessed marriage and family, the kind he writes about. Read ' The Family You Want', and you will be helped!'

Leighton Ford, President, Leighton Ford Ministries,
Charlotte, North Carolina,

'As a pastor, John Huffman ministers amidst the wreckage, grief, hopes and joys of today's assaulted families. His practical wisdom comes from deep personal experience. Here is healing medicine for all care about the family.'

Harold L. Myra, Executive Chairman
Christianity Today International

# The
# Family
# You
# Want

*How to Build an Authentic, Loving Home*

John A. Huffman, Jr.

*[handwritten inscription: Lebanon 2013. To Beth & Peter with all my love and gratitude to God for our friendship.]*

**CHRISTIAN FOCUS**

John Huffman is a husband, father of three daughters, and a pastor. He has served as pastor of the Key Biscayne Presbyterian Church in Florida, the First Presbyterian Church of Pittsburgh in Pennsylvania, and since 1978 has been the senior minister of the St Andrews Presbyterian Church in Newport Beach, California, a 4,700-member congregation. He has written nine books, numerous articles, and has traveled widely as a speaker and as a board member of WorldVision International, Christianity Today International, and Gordon-Conwell Theological Seminary. His wife Anne is a psychoanalyst.

All scripture quotations, unless otherwise indicated, are taken from the HOLY BIBLE, NEW INTERNATIONAL VERSION®. NIV®. Copyright ©1973, 1978, 1984 by International Bible Society. Used by permission of Zondervan. All rights reserved.

© John A. Huffman, Jr.
ISBN 1-85792-933-0

10 9 8 7 6 5 4 3 2 1

Published in 2001
Reprinted 2005
by
Christian Focus Publications Ltd.,
Geanies House, Fearn, Ross-shire,
IV20 1TW, Great Britain

www.christianfocus.com

Cover design by Alister MacInnes
Printed and bound by
CPD, Wales

All rights reserved. No part of this publication may be reproduced, stored in a retrieval system, or transmitted, in any form, by any means, electronic, mechanical, photocopying, recording or otherwise without the prior permission of the publisher or a license permitting restricted copying. In the U.K. such licenses are issued by the Copyright Licensing Agency, 90 Tottenham Court Road, London W1P 9HE.

# Contents

This book is dedicated to
my wife Anne,
my daughters Suzanne, Carla and Janet,
my parents Dorothy and John Huffman and
my in-laws Martha and Crawford Mortensen
and all who have provided my laboratory for
fleshing out this life experience.


And I express my appreciation to
Bill Lobdell, editor, church member and friend
who has given freely of his time and expertise
to make my writing more readable.

# INTRODUCTION

Twenty-seven years ago I wrote a book titled *Becoming a Whole Family*. It represented the best that I had to say as a son, a husband, and a father writing in my early thirties during the early 1970s. At that time, Anne and I lived in Pittsburgh, Pennsylvania. We had two little daughters, five-year-old Suzanne and three-year-old Carla. Anne was a traditional housewife and mother. Richard Nixon was still in the White House.

I am now in my early sixties, writing at the beginning of the 21st Century. Anne and I are now empty-nesters. The youngest of our three daughters, Janet, who was not even born when I wrote the book, is a graduate of the University of the Pacific in Stockton, California, and now in her mid twenties is working back in Newport Beach. Carla, who is a graduate of Stanford University, has worked five years with a law firm in Palo Alto, California, has just completed her MBA in finance and marketing at MIT and is working in the high-tech computer industry with Microsoft in Seattle, Washington. Suzanne, who was our oldest, after graduating from Princeton University in 1990 while battling cancer for 19 months, has now, to our great grief, been dead for almost a decade.

Anne, no longer a traditional housewife and mother, is a highly respected professional who, fifteen years into marriage, entered Fuller Theological Seminary. Over a period of years, she earned two graduate degrees and now has her own psychoanalytic practice here in Newport Beach, California, and serves on the board of her graduate alma mater, Fuller Theological Seminary. As you can tell, there have been some changes in our family in nearly three decades.

Much is different in America, too. The rate of change has been exponential. Although every generation has confronted tragedy, it seems like ours has more than any other – or we see it more closely through the lens of television that now takes us instantly to the most remote places in the world.

CNN and other cable news services are right there on the spot with 24-hour coverage, whether it's a war, a revolution, an earthquake or a hurricane. ESPN brings the latest in sports. And there is even the 24-hour Golf Channel. I carry my cell phone everywhere I go. Faxes have sped up correspondence and, much to the surprise of my technologic-savvy children, I am sitting here at my computer typing e-mails to friends all over the world, even as I edit this book manuscript.

Back in 1973, the idea for that first book on the family emerged from a sermon series that I preached at the First Presbyterian Church in Pittsburgh. At the time, I was quite troubled by something that happened. The messages were enthusiastically received by a substantial segment of the congregation. I noticed that the printed sermon ministry grew from about 300 subscribers to some 3,000 in a matter of those eight weeks. It was that series on the family that pretty well established my printed sermon ministry, which continues to this day. The sermons were replayed each Sunday evening over KDKA radio in Pittsburgh.

At the same time, I noticed a fascinating phenomenon. There were some persons who expressed a strong resistance to my family talk. They urged me to get on with preaching the Bible, to stop wasting time on family concerns. Our attendance dropped off slightly. Some very graciously, but firmly, mentioned that they were single, widowed, or divorced and that such a series was not too helpful to them.

I remember how puzzled I was by these two extreme reactions. Was it, in fact, inappropriate to take valuable Sunday morning time to deal in practical terms with the problems of husband-wife, parent-child relationships? Was it unfair to those who were not – at that point in their lives – married or did not have children to take the time to speak to these unique circumstances? Or should we have reserved such conversation for covenant groups or adult education classes? On the other hand, how could we explain such a tremendous positive response? Some seemed to hunger for more of this biblical-relational preaching.

I discovered the hard way that any talk about family living has to recognize that there are two kinds of families. In those Pittsburgh days, I was aware of one kind of family – the nuclear family – made up of father and mother and whatever number of children they had. The nuclear family is important. We, in the church, need to talk a lot about healthy family relationships. And in fact, at St. Andrew's Presbyterian Church in Newport Beach, California – where I now pastor – the most requested sermon topics all have to do with family themes.

At the same time, we must never forget that there is a second kind of family. This is the extended family. When we talk about family only in nuclear terms of mother-father, parent-child, brother-sister, we have violated our responsibility to relate to every person who needs a family. The widowed, the divorced, the never married – instead of being pushed out of our inner circle of conversation – need to be included. No one is exempt from family concerns unless someone such as myself defines a family in such narrow terms as to intentionally exclude them.

Our society has to give much more attention to the extended family. We have discovered this at St. Andrew's. Some 13,000 persons have now gone through our Divorce Recovery Workshops. That's a staggering statistic. Although only a small percentage of these persons are members of the congregation, our church has reached out into a community that is devastated by divorce. It would be impossible for us today to find a family that has not been touched at least in some way by the horrendous pain of divorce.

Divorce isn't the only thing that creates the need for an extended family. The dynamics of modern life have made us a highly mobile society. Granted, there have been persons all through history who have moved from place to place. Merchants, colonists and members of the military have had a high degree of mobility. However, the highest percentage of society had lived a fairly sedentary existence. But today is quite different from even the 1920s in the United States.

My mother's family, several generations ago, moved from Ontario to Northern Michigan. What little knowledge I have of their immigration was that it was a move involving the extended family. A large number of relatives moved together at one time. They set down their roots in that Northern Michigan farm community and lived there – brothers, sisters, uncles, aunts, cousins – in a place called home. Some would travel on business. Occasionally, one would move to another part of the country. But each knew where his and her roots were.

When my grandmother died back in the mid-1970s, we returned her remains to that community. Her friends and relatives were still there 27 years after she had left them. The uncles and aunts, cousins and their children embraced each other with that ongoing warmth of extended family relationships. When we returned for the memorial service, they greeted my mother, who had left in the mid-1930s, with a warmth and familiarity that astounded me. Now even that community has largely broken up as its young people have moved to other parts of the country.

Our modern life moves so fast! Some of us involved in corporate life go from one city to another every few years. Our children are raised without knowing their cousins. Occasionally they see their grandparents. We are being forced more and more into the nuclear family. Ties are being cut with the extended family.

Christmas of 1995 was the first time in 27 years that our Huffman family had been together for any part of a holiday season. The last time was in 1968 when our nuclear family included my father and mother, my sister and her husband, and Anne and me. Even then, the three component parts – my parents, my sister's family and my family – lived in three different parts of the country. It took the wedding of my nephew in Southern California to get us all together. This time, those six original members of our nuclear family had more than tripled in number, with cousins who hadn't seen each other for years finally getting together. Children were reunited with their grandparents. We are being forced more and more into the nuclear family as geographical separation cuts our ties with the extended family. I hardly know the names and geographic locations of the children of my cousins.

Then add to that divorce with all of its implications, and we see the need for a broader understanding of family. The family is not just father-mother, brother-sister, parent-child. The family extends to all those who are part of a blood relationship. In addition, the extended family reaches out to include other relationships that we have in our communities.

The church is a family. It is the family of God. It is a community of individuals who cannot go it alone, who need each other. Therefore, when we talk about family, it is important to understand that church is just as much a family in its responsibilities to care for each other as are our own nuclear families.

So if you are single, widowed or divorced, I apologize for any truncated, individualistic understanding the church has shared about family living that does not show there's a place for you. There is a place for you in the people of God, the family of Jesus Christ. God did not create you to go it alone in this world. The Old Testament has a magnificent statement in Psalm 68:5-6a, which reads:

A father to the fatherless, a defender of widows, is God in his holy dwelling. God sets the lonely in families....

Never forget those verses. God is in the business of bringing together families, both nuclear and extended. He created a family where we have our blood relationships. He created the church to be a family of believers. God knows that we are social beings. God knows we cannot go it alone. So he created various kinds of families to help meet our basic social needs.

So, I've written this new book. It reaffirms much of what I wrote in the early 1970s when I was in my early 30s. But there is so much more to say. Life seems to have accelerated in its pace. It certainly is much more complex. Circumstances have changed. I've interacted with and counseled so many more people in the intervening years. And I have done so much more living myself.

Here is the best of my thinking, coming from a more seasoned veteran of family living. I hope you will find it helpful!

*God sets the lonely in families...*

Psalm 68:6a.

So just what is a family?

I have cast around looking for metaphors of family living. The best I have come up with is that of a mobile. You have seen mobiles. Probably the most common is the one that dangles over a baby's crib.

Question: Is a mobile singular or plural? Answer: Well, it's both, isn't it? It is one object made up of many parts.

Question: Is a mobile static or dynamic? Answer: Well, if there is not much air movement in the room, it is reasonably static. At times it appears to dangle in a fixed position. However, all you have to do is open or close the door quickly, and the breeze that creates makes for a dynamic interrelation of those miscellaneous parts.

Question: Is a mobile sturdy or fragile? Answer: In most cases, it is very fragile, is it not? Much of the time, elements of a mobile settle into a reasonably stable relationship with each other. But aided by nothing more than a mild breeze or a swipe of a baby's hand and the mobile can move with frantic energy, which has enormous potential for those fragile threads to become tangled or even severed.

A family can be thought of as a living mobile made up of human personalities. It is a work of art that takes many years to produce but is never finished. The framework of a family gives it form. A family has movement. It is constantly in motion. There is freedom within limits. There is never any one day in which two persons in the family are at the same point of growth.

Each one is developing. Each one is in relationship to the others. Each one is developing socially, intellectually, physically, and spiritually. Every person in the family has an effect upon the other members in all these areas. Over a period of years these fragile strings strengthen into strong, invisible steel that holds great weight but is also capable of an enormous amount of freedom.

Families can be dysfunctional. Many are. In fact, I am convinced that all of us, to one extent or another, are dysfunctional persons coming from dysfunctional families who, in turn, will create some degree of dysfunction in the families we establish. I'll have more to say about this later.

In its most positive form, the family can be a place of increased individual and corporate wholeness. Whether it is a nuclear family or an extended family, it is individuals, created with unique potential in the image of God, living in relationship with each other. There is a place for you no matter how old you are or how young you are, no matter what is your status of life. The New King James Version of the Bible translates Psalm 68:6a in this way: 'God sets the solitary in families.' This means that God is the security of all. He is the protector of the defenseless. He gives you a home. He offers you a family. You don't have to go it alone!

Keeping the picture of a mobile in mind, let us take a look at the supportive functions that a family provides.

Dr. Ted Ward, formerly of Michigan State University and Trinity Seminary in the Chicago area, points out that the family has three specific functions.

First, the family has a *coping* function.
It is protective. We see this most particularly in relationship to children. A family shelters, teaches, and launches a person. A family helps the individual, both child and adult, become more competent to deal with social realities. The very way we

are held, fed by bottle or breast, talked to, prayed for, nurtured or not nurtured has a profound future impact on how we view ourselves and others. Healthy parenting provides a secure base of acceptance. It provides a secure base of acceptance from which an individual can move out into the world. We achieve competence. We become better able to reach out.

Look at the most basic coping functions a family provides in relationship to a little baby. Look at how we protect that baby. The family hovers around the infant. It tries to meet that child's every need. It does for a one-year-old what it wouldn't consider doing for an eight-year-old.

The same is true in the church. A new-born person in Jesus Christ must be protected by the family. We help that person grow. We urge that one on in his or her development. We change the dirty diapers. We teach them how to eat the Bread of Life. All this is done within this caring community called the family of God. We protect each other. That is why God sets the lonely in families. We need to protect each other.

In the healthy, nuclear family, the physical provisions of food, shelter, and clothing are made. These are undergirded by the additional emotional and spiritual encouragements that help us survive as social persons. A healthy church becomes the family of God to us, supplementing and complementing contributions of a good home and helping us to make good the deficiencies of a poor home. They help us cope with life, enabling us to live in community.

There is a second function called *modeling*.
You cannot simply be protective, sheltering a person forever. We learn from watching other persons. Therefore, both in the nuclear and extended families, those who are more mature serve as models to help the younger ones learn how to live. Give a person the wrong model, and you are in trouble. An indolent mother or alcoholic father sets a pattern for a young person that is difficult to break. A church filled with bickering people teaches young Christians how to be brittle, offensive, defensive,

hard in their Christian life. If your role model is hostile, you may pick up some of those hostility patterns yourself. If your role model is loving, you will see that as an ideal to be emulated. However, there is one big problem. If we see family relationships built primarily on the basis of modeling, we can end up being the carbon copy of someone else.

Unfortunately, I have seen this happen in too many situations. We as ministers can be the most guilty of trying to mold others into exact replicas of ourselves. Instead of producing maturity in others within the family relationship, we can actually destroy a person's ability to stand on his own two feet. Carry a baby everywhere, never encouraging that baby to exercise and to begin to get a sense of balance, and you will delay the child's ability to walk.

This brings us to a third function, the *developmental* function. The family must protect the coping function. The family must model. However, the family must move beyond being the protective cocoon and the arbitrary inculcation that tells another person what to do in all situations. We need to encourage people in their own developmental maturity.

How sad it is to see a person who has been programmed to think and respond in particular ways that might work in some settings. However, place that person in a different environment and their mechanically learned ways of doing things can backfire. The mother, the father, the pastor, the teacher is no longer there to help them process the many options and even temptations. They've not been encouraged to understand their own individuality and appreciate their own unique gifts. They've been programmed to respond in memorized ways that, in some settings, work very well. In other settings, some of these memorized routines might backfire.

A mature person is someone who understands why they are acting in certain ways, understanding the negative or positive long-range consequences of behaviors or attitudes.

I have a friend who was spiritually raped by his mother. I

know that is strong language. I am convinced, though, that that is exactly what happened. God was portrayed as an arbitrary, judgmental, unloving parental figure who wanted to squeeze all the fun and joy out of life. As hard as he tries, my friend has never quite recovered from this negative approach to the Christian faith. He has never been able to see Jesus Christ in a context larger than the harshly defined negativity so awesomely inflicted upon him and his brother by an overbearing mother who wanted to be in control at all times. Instead of leading him to a God bigger than her, she inadvertently became the personification of that God in frightening ways. She struck out, failing to provide that total ministry that was her privileged responsibility.

Some families fail to render this developmental function. In such situations, it might take years of therapy, emotional and spiritual, to undo the damage of a well-meaning family that has provided adequate coping and modeling mechanisms but has failed to teach a growing child or Christian how to function without the arbitrary, artificial support of mother and father and other parental figures in the church.

What I am trying to say is this: whether it is in the nuclear family or the extended family, we can produce automatons. We can create mechanical men and women who live their lives in protective wombs. We can tell people what to do, making their decisions for them and failing to encourage them into mature lifestyles. There are rules. The Bible specifies certain conduct that is appropriate and inappropriate for the believer. Moses outlines specifically how we are to live a life in relationship with God, modeling it for our families.

Moses wrote in Deuteronomy 6:6-9:

These commandments that I give you today are to be upon your hearts. Impress them on your children. Talk about them when you sit at home and when you walk along the road, when you lie down and when you get up. Tie them as symbols on your hands and bind them on your foreheads. Write them on the door frames of your houses and on your gates.

However, there is this additional dimension of a developmental ministry in which we stand by our loved ones at the point of their disequilibration. We must not make it too easy or they will not develop into mature persons. The Apostle Paul kept calling for maturity. He urges us as follows in Ephesians 4:12-14:

> ... to prepare God's people for works of service, so that the body of Christ may be built up until we all reach unity in the faith and in the knowledge of the Son of God and become mature, attaining to the whole measure of the fullness of Christ. Then we will no longer be infants, tossed back and forth by the waves, and blown here and there by every wind of teaching and by the cunning and craftiness of men in their deceitful scheming.

I think we see this disequilibration most specifically illustrated in the life of a young person who grows up in a Christian family and church. That young person then becomes exposed to higher education, perhaps in a secular university. We could create a cocoon that never exposes this young person to the world. We protect. We could model and not allow this young adult to interact with the outside world. When young people have doubts we could shame them into not pursuing those areas, restricting instead of encouraging. We can come through with our easy answers to very complex questions, not allowing them to work through their own problem within a caring family.

My sister Miriam and I will forever be grateful to our mother and father for allowing us to express our doubts at home. We knew where mother and dad stood. We still know where they stand. They had protected us and helped us cope with the very basics of human existence. They had modeled for us. But they also entered into this third dimension, which is so important. They helped us walk through our problems as we made the transition from childhood to adulthood, not forcing on us easy, packaged answers. They knew that there were some questions that we had to resolve ourselves. They were willing to gradually let their roles as parents evolve as they encouraged our roles as children to evolve into adulthood. They were willing to re-linquish their dominance in a way that enabled us to become equals with them as adults.

Most of us are familiar with transactional analysis. Simply stated, this psychological model notes that some of us try to function perpetually as parents. We want to tell other people what to do. Some of us are children in certain relationships. We allow people to tell us what to do. Some of us have emerged, at least in selected areas, into adulthood where we are capable of making decisions, providing leadership that is freed from external domination. We are becoming whole persons as God created us to be, ready to assume responsibility.

We need to learn from nature. Picture that mother bird who so carefully prepared a soft, cushioned nest. Picture those eggs kept warm by her body. See those eggs at the appropriate time begin to break forth and tiny little birds emerging. Observe the mother as she tenderly cares for their every need, providing food, liquid, protection. Then what is observed? The moment comes, that moment of disequilibration in which the mother instinc-tively knows that the nestlings cannot live forever dependent upon her. Finally she pushes them out of the nest, urging them to feel their own wings so that finally they can fly.

Too often, as both mothers and fathers in the home and leaders in the church, we negate the personhood of others. We can meet our own neurotic needs by encouraging dependency relationships. We can try to subjugate others to us instead of encouraging them to move beyond us into the exciting dynamics of what God is doing through his Holy Spirit.

God has set us in families. He has given us the privilege to function in that mobile of independent interrelatedness. He wants us to be protectors, modelers, encouragers. That's what a family is. That's why we have families. God help us fulfill these privileged responsibilities in a world that needs men and women who are not scripted to simply parent others or be perpetual children but to be adults who have learned to spread our wings and fly, while continuing to live in healthy interrelationship with each other.

# Chapter 2
## There Are No Perfect Families

*We know that the whole creation has been groaning as in the pains of childbirth right up to the present time. Not only so, but we ourselves, who have the first fruits of the Spirit, groan inwardly as we wait eagerly for our adoption as sons and daughters, the redemption of our bodies. For in this hope we were saved. But hope that is seen is no hope at all. Who hopes for what he already has?*

Romans 8:22-24

In the late 1960s and early 1970s I would often begin a preaching mission or a family retreat with two disturbing quotes about the future of the family as we then knew it.

The first quote was from Ferdinand Lundberg, author of *The Coming World Transformation*, stating that the family is: '...near the point of complete extinction.'

The second quote came from psychoanalyst William Wolf who declared, 'The family is dead except for the first year or two of child raising. This will be its only function.'

Then I would add an observation by sociologist Margaret Mead who then predicted that within 50 years the family, as we know it, would no longer exist.

These were considered to be highly pessimistic predictions. I used them to capture the attention of people, knowing that many would protest such quotations as brash overstatements.

I was attacked by those who protested about such pessimistic predictions coming from the mouth of a minister of the Gospel of Jesus Christ. Those who were much more optimistic genuinely predicted that the family was in for a 'golden age'. They were declaring that, with a society moving toward increased leisure time, families would be able to spend more time together, deriving satisfaction from shared activities. The old slogan, 'The family that prays together stays together', was revised to say, 'The family that *plays* together stays together!'

I wish those who argued with me back then had proven to be right. I took no joy in such pessimistic predictions. But frankly, the last quarter of a century has validated such concerns.

Our associate pastor, Bill Flanagan, has given careful research to the tragic increase in statistics of family breakdown. He writes:

> Divorce is always a tragedy, no matter how civilized our handling of it may be. It is always a confession and outgrowth of human failure, even when it is the sorry better of sorry alternatives.
>
> The divorce rate has risen 700 percent this century. Approximately one-half of first marriages are doomed to failure. More than one million children a year are involved in divorce cases.
>
> More than thirteen million children under 18 have one or both parents missing. Within three years after the divorce decree, half of the fathers never see their children. Single-parent families are growing at 20 times the rate of two-parent families.
>
> Between 1960 and 1975, the divorce rate increased 130 percent. During the decade of the 70s, divorce rates more than doubled. Through the 1980s to the present, it has remained constant at about 50 percent. In other words, half of all marriages will end in a broken relationship.
>
> More than 70 percent of these persons remarry within three years, and 65 percent of the new marriages will fail again. Those that marry a third time have a failure rate of 75 percent.

Flanagan adds these additional statistics: Within the United States over one-fifth of all the families are single-parent households. More than 25 million children are in these homes, and this number is increasing at approximately one million a year. There are now more than 13 million blended families that are incorporating their children from former marriages into new households. If you really want to be staggered by tough statistics, 55-60 percent of the children in the Los Angeles public school district are being raised in single-parent families.

We are also seeing an epidemic of divorce even among clergy families. Although I've never drawn any attention to this, at any given time at St. Andrew's we will have two or three former clergy spouses attending anonymously, hoping to continue their walk with the Lord in the safety of this large community of faith.

Dr. Howard Hendricks of Dallas Theological Seminary notes how capable we all are of making a mess in our family relationships. Specifically, he was referring to clergy persons such as myself when he stated: 'Any man with a little bit of money, a Christian education, and some popularity can with great style make a mess out of his marriage.'

It is only when you and I confront our own potential to mess up our relationships that we are set free by God's grace to work at them in a way that moves against these pessimistic statistics of our day, creating a God-anointed, realistic, proactive optimism.

As a pastor of persons, I see first-hand where people are struggling in their relationships, and here are some of the big issues that come up again and again when they seek help in trying to repair their broken families.

*Spousal abuse* is often an issue. How sad it is to hear the story of a woman (or, in some cases, a man) who has been, with great frequency, emotionally and/or physically beaten.

*Substance abuse*, in its various forms such as alcoholism and drug usage, hammers away at the very heart of a family relationship.

*Mental illness*, in all its manifestations, is another problem confronting families with greater frequency. The psychotic actions of a child, the increased frequency of deep, life-threatening depression, manic depression, and various forms of psychopathology can put tremendous strain on the most loving family relationships.

*Gambling addiction* is raising its ugly head more often as our society has gradually dropped its restraints against this activity which devastates families. The seductive nature of legalized gambling and even state-run lotteries encourages the compulsion, which becomes a disease for some.

*Sexual addiction* has always been with us but has become more pervasive in its impact on the family. Those of us who would never have considered wandering into the red-light district of sleazy porno shops and massage parlors cannot peruse even the non-pay TV channels of a typical hotel room today without confronting highly erotic, soft-core pornography. The neighborhood video store makes available every kind of voyeuristic opportunity to those of all age levels. The typical Hollywood film cannot succeed without implicit and most often explicit activity that encourages our societal preoccupation with distorted sexuality. And the Internet brings every kind of pornography imaginable – and some unimaginable – directly into our family.

Let's not kid ourselves. None of us who is a healthy human being is exempt from such temptations to fantasize and to act out those fantasies in ways destructive to the family. If that's not enough, think of how incest, venereal disease and sexual harassment in the workplace compound the already tragic consequences of sexual sin. We see ourselves living in a society that has gone crazy sexually. With increasing frequency, persons who have discovered their spouse's unfaithfulness are, in counseling, confiding in me that they have been tested for AIDS. They are fearful of what their spouse might bring home to them.

*Careerism* is another compulsion of our era. At one time we bowed to it as the American capitalistic ethic. But now we see it for what it is. We often find both partners consumed selfishly with their careers, perhaps initially sucked into workaholic lifestyles by the realities of providing economically for their families in a tough environment. But ultimately they succumb to materialism and self-centeredness.

It used to be that the church could talk about these issues as 'out there', and if you come to Jesus and become a member of his church, you'll be set free from such realities. Frankly, I am convinced that even in the best of times that attitude was one of *denial*. The facts are that all through human history these issues have been with us. Even the person who, with God's help, is living a life that closely conforms to the positive standards of God's Word cannot guarantee a life exempt from being impacted by a spouse, children, or parents who are engaged in these family-threatening attitudes and activities.

In more than 35 years of ministry, I've witnessed this scene too often: An apparently caring, sensitive person comes to me with a sad story of a once-trusted spouse who has declared, 'I no longer love you, and I've found someone who is better for me at this stage of my life.' And, in the era of easy no-fault divorce, the mate has literally walked off from the marriage.

When I use my Sunday message to talk about family issues, it usually stirs up deep emotions within the congregation. On one particular Sunday, a woman came up to me after church with an impassioned expression, pleading with me to address the issue of incest. Obviously she saw the nonplused look on my face, which said, 'I'm not certain I'm prepared to tackle that issue.' It's a tough one, isn't it? To emphasize her point, she wrote me a letter, which I received later that week. The letter read:

I spoke with you after services this morning about being an incest survivor and requesting that you address the issue.

John, my life has been tormented by my father's abuses that spanned five years of my childhood. My father was not an ignorant man; he was the founding senior partner of a Wall St. law firm! He spoke five languages and was a devoted 'religious' man. He attended the seminary and 'knew' God's Word. I was raped, tortured, and destroyed by him.

My life is full of joy today; however, it was not always this way. I did not resemble the 'nice' girl from an upper middle class home in my teens and twenties. I've been promiscuous, because that's the way I was taught to be. I've had three abortions out of fear of doing to a child what was done to me. I've been anything but the Christian God wanted me to be, because my earthly father violated my soul and then went to church. It's been very hard to accept that my Father in heaven loved me after letting my earthly father destroy my innocence. Accepting Christ and His Father have been the single hardest challenge in my life!

One in four women is incested in the U.S., and it happens in 'nice' Newport Beach homes as well as Watts. I know it's difficult to preach about such an emotionally charged issue. John, I pray and beg that you will be strong enough to bring this issue out of the darkness and into the light of God's presence. I pray because there are 25 percent of the children in the homes of our congregation who are being violated *right now!* Please help to save them from the pain and torment of my life by keeping us, as the adults, accountable for their protection. I want my story to be the last of its kind.

So I've cataloged for you the list of the big, horrendous issues that confront us today. I trust I've made the point that not even Christian families are exempt from trouble as we increasingly hear of persons who leave their marriage vows, declaring, 'I have the right to be me.'

How sad it is to realize that there are couples active in Christian churches who lead undetected double lives until finally an explosion comes that separates them from the community of believers, which had not been of much help to them in coping with their problems. At St. Andrew's, we've started covenant groups, seminars, counseling and preaching that we hope are of some use. We have referred many couples to long-term counseling, which in many cases has been helpful.

But there are families whose problems never surface to public view. They keep attending services. They serve on church boards. They make their public professions of faith. Still, there are those internal disruptions they can't handle. They go on leading private lives of great pain. One friend of mine refers to their condition as 'not bad enough for divorce but not good enough to be called a marriage.'

Some of these issues are so great that they eventually lead to the brokenness of divorce. Some of these problems don't end up in divorce. However, they cause enormous hurt within the family as people violated by others struggle with emotional, spiritual and physical anguish, trying to make sense out of life as a result of the pain they've experienced in past family relationships. This makes it difficult to maintain healthful relationships within their new family structures, either nuclear or extended.

Every *unhealthy* family has issues. And every *healthy* family has them too. That's right. Even healthy families have problems. The question is, 'What will we do with them?'

At St. Andrew's we have had thousands of persons go through our premarital seminars. In these seminars, we talk proactively about the possibility of Christian marriage. We take as the starting point for our first group premarital session the reality that something at the very core of our human existence is out of kilter. We talk about the reality of human sin and the biblical truth that none of us is perfect. We try to get across the fact that if none of us is perfect then there is no such thing as a perfect marriage. Even the best of marriages has its issues – because people, individually, have issues. Marriages are made up of people.

Early in my ministry, it used to be that some of the couples were irritated by my discussion of such problems. After all, their eyes were aglow with love. They often commented to each other, 'Isn't it amazing how much we have in common, how we enjoy the same things, how much we think alike?' However, I've discovered in the last ten or fifteen years that much of this optimism has disappeared. Couples come to the altar more tentatively, having observed the broken lives of their

own families and friends and the larger society. I am discovering a much greater receptivity to objective discussions about
the issues in marriage than I used to sense. I pray that most
of you reading this book are not dealing, right now, with the
horrendous nature of some of these big issues of which I've
written. But I do know all of us are dealing with some of the
following issues that I'd like to address just briefly as I do in
the premarital seminar.

Let me mention a few of the potential problem areas that
every marriage faces. You may discover that you are not alone
in encountering several of these areas yourself.

Issue one: *Differences in family background.*
No two people come from an identical home environment.
Adjustments in this area may be minimal if the couple grew up
in the same town, went to the same school, attended the same
church, joined the same clubs, and had fathers and mothers
engaged in similar employment. This is seldom the case in our
increasingly mobile world. Forty years ago many an engaged
couple had the benefit of knowing each other in their childhood
years or were aware of each other in high school or college. Today the majority meet in the marketplace without the benefit
of having ever observed each other in their natural habitat of
nuclear and extended family.

For example, Art meets Karen four years out of college. She is
from the Northeast. He is from the Midwest. They both moved
to California because of work opportunities. She was raised in
a Congregational church. He is Roman Catholic. Both dropped
out of church during college. Her father is a successful corporate
lawyer on his second marriage. Her mother, once a homemaker,
is now a single woman pursuing a master's degree in art history. His father is a foreman in a factory, and his mother works
as a teller in a bank. Art and Karen love each other very much.
They met at a singles' bar where they were instantly attracted
to each other. They dress similarly. They enjoy the same type
of entertainment. They majored in college in similar subjects.

The marketplace serves as a melting pot, bringing them together in apparent oneness. They date, fall in love, and plan to get married. Before they announce their engagement, they briefly meet each other's parents, and it becomes official. They plan a wedding, struggling with whether to go back to her hometown and transport his family in for the event or to bring the whole group out to California where their most-recent friends reside. They get married in California.

Then come the problems. Karen was raised with unlimited credit cards at her disposal. Art doesn't believe in extended credit. His family paid cash on the line to make sure they had enough money to make ends meet. Although neither of them has been to church for some time, they feel they should prob-ably give some attention to religious matters for the sake of future children. Karen is nostalgic about the simplicity of her Congregational style of worship. Art misses the liturgy of the Roman Catholic church. Karen's mother wants her to become a member of the Junior League. Art's family has never heard of the organization. Karen prefers gourmet cooking. Art's real preference is Southern fried chicken with mashed potatoes and gravy. The two love each other very much. They are just different. These differences can cause trouble.

Issue two: *Problems within in-laws.*
One of the biggest crises in the newlyweds' life is deciding in which parents' home they will spend their first Christmas. Lit-tle did they anticipate this could be a problem. Both families are sentimental about holidays. They have their own timeworn customs. Both naturally envision the couple opening their gifts with them around their Christmas tree. Art and Karen now live in Los Angeles. They are aspiring to come up with the down payment for a house a few miles away in Santa Monica. Should they go to her parents in Boston to be with her dad and his new family? Or should they go to be with her mother? Or do they go to his parents in Peoria? Do they accept the two plane tickets from her father or do they rob from their savings and buy dis-

count tickets to be with her mother or his parents? Or do they disappoint all of the parents and stay here, feeling lonely and cut off from their roots?

When will they open their presents? Karen always did this on Christmas Eve after the family Christmas Eve service. Art cannot understand that. 'What are they, greedy or something? Can't they postpone immediate gratification for opening them at the right time, which is Christmas morning?' He remembers those tingling sensations of coming home from midnight mass, being tucked away in bed, and then coming down the stairs at the crack of dawn to see what was under the Christmas tree.

Then there is the problem with Karen's sister who had originally moved out and temporarily roomed with her but now is living with her boyfriend in Westwood. If they do stay here for Christmas, she wants to come with him. They don't like him, don't approve of the living arrangement, and feel that if she comes alone, that's fine. They don't want to appear to be approving of this living arrangement.

Issue three: *The problem of money.*
Every couple I know has either too little or too much. You say you can't have too much? Perhaps not. I have never yet seen a couple who felt they had too much. Although I have known a few who have. How do you handle what you do have? How do you make it stretch? How do you decide the priorities? Is it a new car or furniture for the living room? Who handles the checkbook? Do you both write checks on the same account? What if he forgets to write down a check when you are meticulous in keeping the checkbook balanced? Every person has a money personality. Either you are a spendthrift or a miser. You say, 'That seems a bit exaggerated.' No, it is not. Because two misers married to each other will not be identical in their miserly ways. One will seem like a spendthrift to the other. Two spendthrifts will find that one seems miserly compared to the other.

Issue four: *Religion.*
As wonderful as it is, nothing can cause more trouble. Who decides what church? Must both hold the same theological views? What about the parents who insist that their grandchildren be raised Roman Catholic while the other in-laws are dyed-in-the-wool Presbyterians, Pentecostals, or Reformed Jews?

Issue five: *Differing temperaments.*
He likes to ski. She is into ceramics. She likes parties. He prefers an evening in front of a TV watching sports. She talks a lot. He is more introverted.

Issue six: *Habits.*
She smokes. He opposes it. He thought he could talk her into stopping. She doesn't like his little sermons.

Issue seven: *The matter of children.*
Do we have any? How many? How do we raise them? One insists on being strict. The other wants their child to have the same kind of carefree, happy youth he/she had.

Issue eight: *Then there is sex.*
It seems like that's all he thinks about at 10:30 every night, but he doesn't give it much attention when he comes home at 6:30 and complains that dinner is not ready. He settles in behind a newspaper, a magazine, or sits for three hours in front of the TV trying to recoup from a hard day. She has worked too and may even make more money than he does but is expected to clean the apartment, cook the meals, and do the laundry. He will take out the trash, occasionally do some shopping, but not much more. He sees her as sexually unresponsive. She sees him as insensitive to a woman's need for tenderness and words of endearment.

There are many more issues. *Ageing parents* present economic and time constraints on some families at very inconvenient times. There can be a *physical illness* or an *emotional breakdown* or *the death of a child.* And there can be the *too-high expectations of one's marriage partner!*

We can go on listing the potential problems in marriage, those we mentioned plus the many more. They would discourage the most optimistic soul. However, you and I are being totally unrealistic if we hide our heads in the sand when it comes to family issues. Perhaps, right now, you are confronted with one or more of these as a young couple. You are discouraged. You are bewildered. Perhaps you are older. You have had your children, and they are out on their own. Now you discover how much you have grown apart during these years. Perhaps yours is a second marriage. He has three children by his first wife and has raised them. You have never been married before. You want your own child. He didn't express any opposition to the idea before you got married. Now he is not interested in starting over again and has warned you not to 'trick' him into it. Issues come in all shapes and sizes. I list these only to help you realize that your difficulties are not unique to you.

Why do we have these issues? There actually is an answer to that question. That is what the church of Jesus Christ is most equipped to give!

There are those who would like to solve issues confronting American families with sociological and psychological answers. Both can be helpful. But at the core is the deep theological reality of human dysfunctionality, sin and imperfection. There were those theological liberals who, at the turn of this past century, declared the twentieth century would be the 'Christian Century'. World War I was supposed to be 'the war to end all wars'. Then came the Depression, World War II, six million Jews killed, the Nazi Holocaust, Stalinist purges, the Cold War, the Vietnam War, the fall of the Iron Curtain, only to expose a world of tribalism and multiple holocausts. Far from getting better, as the Social Darwinists predicted, our great technological advance has left us in a bigger mess than we ever have been in before. Not only are we seeing a breakdown in the family, but also we are seeing a world in ecological disarray and a world in which the most trusted have been discredited by scandal.

That's what the Apostle Paul is declaring when he writes: I consider that our present sufferings are not worth comparing with the glory that will be revealed in us. The creation waits in eager expectation for the sons of God to be revealed. For the creation was subjected to frustration, not by its own choice, but by the will of the one who subjected it, in hope that the creation itself will be liberated from its bondage to decay and brought into the glorious freedom of the children of God.

We know that the whole creation has been groaning as in the pains of childbirth right up to the present time (Rom. 8:18-22).

In the same way, the Spirit helps us in our weakness. We do not know what we ought to pray for, but the Spirit himself intercedes for us with groans that words cannot express. And he who searches our hearts knows the mind of the Spirit, because the Spirit intercedes for the saints in accordance with God's will (Rom. 8:26-27).

There are answers. They come from the Bible. I beg you not to dismiss this theological understanding without giving it a fair hearing. This theological/biblical understanding of why families have issues addresses people who would be optimistic, falsely believing that our marriages can be perfect. It also speaks directly to those who would be pessimistic and see a continuing downward spiral in our society, making men and women distrustful of the possibility of personal commitment and of family relationships, either nuclear or extended.

The Bible gives a straightforward explanation that helps us understand some of the dilemmas we experience, and how to work through them. I call it an *optimistic/pessimistic/optimistic* understanding of the family, both nuclear and extended.

That's what we mean when we talk about a *theology of creation*. God has great dreams for us, entrusting to Adam and Eve the stewardship of his earthly creation, entrusting to humankind ecological responsibility. The Bible describes us being created in the very image of God with the capacity to make moral choices. God drew a line, a somewhat arbitrary line, designed for the welfare of humankind. He warned what would happen if we aspired to be God instead of realizing our highest potential as human beings – living in loving and caring relationship with each other and in a loving and caring relationship with God. This makes me optimistic!

The Bible sketches for us a *theology of the fall*. That's the beginning of trouble. That's where problems come into this world. Issues multiply. The first man and woman stepped across the line. They aspired to be like God. They bought Satan's whispered promises. They thought they knew better than God did, and you and I have been doing it ever since, selfishly thinking we know best. Fallen humankind is selfish. Selfishness destroys relationships. Fallen humankind plays God, creating an environment in which each person does what is right in his/her own eyes.

We have a term for that. The word is anarchy. I want what I want, and I am going to get it on my terms when I want to get it. You want what you want, and you are going to get it on your terms when you want to get it. On that basis, we are going to have a tough time getting along with each other in society, aren't we? When I want what I want, and I'm going to get it no matter what, and you want what you want, and you are going to get it no matter what, and if I'm married to you, we are going to have real trouble in the nuclear family. This makes me pessimistic!

The doctrine of creation gives us a sense of optimism about the family, both nuclear and extended. So the doctrine of the fall, when taken seriously, gives us a spirit of pessimism about the nuclear and extended family. There is very little room for hope. But this is not the end of the story.

The Bible sketches for us a *theology of redemption*. This describes the potential restoration of humankind created in the image of God – now fallen, broken, and alienated – into a new creation. This word was first promised by God to Adam and Eve when they were thrust out of the idyllic garden. Their work, which was originally the crowning glory of their function, now took on the element of thorn, thistle and sweat. God promised that One would come who would crush the head of the serpent. That One has come. His name is Jesus Christ. He experienced everything you and I experience, yet without sin. He took upon himself our sins on the cross that we might die to sin and live to righteousness.

He calls us to bring our issues to him. He wants to forgive us and give us a new beginning. He wants to restore us. Through the energy of his Holy Spirit, he wants to empower us to realize His original intention in creation. This makes me optimistic!

That's why I say, mine, as a Christian, is an *optimistic/pessimistic/optimistic* view of the family. It is pessimistic in that I understand the reality of Jesus' teaching – that in this world we will have trouble. I also understand his teachings take us at face value, inviting us to bring our problems to him, experiencing his forgiveness, finding his healing and restoration in a way that binds us together with him in our vertical relationship and to work creatively in our horizontal relationships with each other. This perspective declares that we live in the 'not yet', in the 'in-between'.

Our redemption is secure in Jesus Christ, even as we await that day when he shall return and set all things right. In the meantime, we are privileged to have his help to be all he dreams of us being in the very midst of serious problems, self-imposed and imposed by others. No one else has the power to destroy you as you open yourself vulnerably to the God of all creation. He then protects you even as you open yourself vulnerably, with all of your issues, to those you love.

# CHAPTER 3

# WHAT JESUS CHRIST CAN DO FOR YOUR FAMILY

*If we claim to be without sin, we deceive ourselves and the truth is not in us. If we confess our sins, he is faithful and just and will forgive us our sins and purify us from all unrighteousness. If we claim we have not sinned, we make him out to be a liar and his word has no place in our lives.*

1 John 1:8-10

We hear a lot about the breakdown in family living. We confront a lot of cynicism about marriage. It is important to note that marriage rates do steadily decline here in the United States. In 1970, married couples occupied 71 percent of U.S. households. By 1994, the figure was only 55 percent. Almost one-third of all children born now in the United States are born to single mothers.

However there is a different angle to this story that needs to be told. Kathleen Kelleher, writing in the *Los Angeles Times*, declares:

*Warning:* Being single may be hazardous to your health.

Decades of study show that – statistically, anyway – marriage leads to a longer, happier life.

She goes on to note that married people tend to eat better, earn more, take better care of themselves and handle stress better than those who are divorced, widowed or never wed.

John Mirowsky, a psychology professor at Ohio State University, states: 'The mutual commitment and long-term partnership is of major value emotionally.' He goes on to say, 'The married also have fewer headaches, stomachaches, back pains and sick days.'

University of Chicago sociologist Linda J. Waite and USC economist Lee Lillard note in another study that married men who make it to age 48 have an 86 percent shot of hitting 65 years of age, 25 percent higher than never-married men. Widowers and divorced men have 67 and 63 percent chances, respectively. Married women who live to age 48 stand an 84 percent chance of making it to 65, 23 percent more than never-married women. Widows and divorced women have 80 and 63 percent chances, respectively.

In his book *The Masculine Self*, Chris Kilmartin declares that bachelors are hospitalized three times and divorced men eight times more often than married men. Men by nature tend to deny emotions and don't have the depth of friendships that women do. The very fact of being married to a woman and talking about your problems has a beneficial effect on your mental health and, by extension, physical health.

Women have some additional stress because of marriage, such as child care. But, in spite of the 'Florence Nightingale/Martha Stewart' complex, married women are also healthier in body and mind than unmarried women.

That's good news for those of us committed to marriage and family living. So how can Jesus Christ help?

A somewhat cynical fellow, hearing me talk positively about Jesus Christ and family living, threw these startling words at me:

All this religious talk sounds nice – that is, if you are religious. But I dare you show me one practical thing your Jesus can do for me and my messed-up family situation. Don't just say a pious prayer and walk on. Show me something real!

Being confronted with that kind of challenge, I was forced to do some thinking.

We've already acknowledged that the family is under attack. Soaring divorce rates make it clear that it's tougher to survive in family living today than a generation ago.

I have to be honest enough to raise the question myself. Does Jesus Christ minister only to the spiritual side of our lives? Or does he make a contribution to the complicated business of family living?

I am convinced that Jesus Christ is capable, available, and ready to do many things for you and your family if you let him.

Let's take a look at several.

First, *Jesus Christ can give you help outside of your own resources.*
If there is one miracle he performs every day, it is creating new people. I don't mean just releasing a person like yourself to brand-new dimensions of human experience. He also does that. One of the greatest contributions Jesus Christ can make to your family is to give your family a new you. Wouldn't it be something if you could suddenly be remade?

Imagine the transformation your family would have if your husband had a brand-new wife, if your wife had a brand-new husband, if your children had a brand-new father or brand-new mother, or if your parents had a brand-new son or daughter. How exciting it would be to be released from some of the conditioned reflexes, negative drags, and limited thought patterns that box us in! That is precisely what Christ wants to do for you. The Bible says, 'Therefore, if anyone is in Christ, he is a new creation; the old has gone, the new has come!' (2 Cor. 5:17). God is in the business of recreating you. That's why some people talk about being born again. Others talk about a new life in Christ. Still others refer to being transformed by God's Spirit.

Unfortunately, many people come to church trying to find insights into Christian living who don't even qualify to be called Christians. If you endeavor to live life more creatively as a result of your faithful church attendance, you are in for an existence of increasing frustration. You are engaged in what the Bible calls 'a form of godliness which denies the power thereof' (2 Tim. 3:5). Jesus Christ sets an enormously high standard for living. Try to mimic him, try to apply his teachings to your life without being remade by him, and you will ultimately come to a point of despair. His standard is so high that your own human abilities fall short of reaching that height of perfectionism. You can even hurt your family by trying to be a better person in your own strength. You can become bogged down with guilt as a result of your failures. Your high aspirations will never be reached. Your pattern of falling short will tear you apart.

One of my good friends has experienced both of these realities. He was raised in a religious home. Both his grandmother and his father were elders in a Presbyterian Church. He dutifully attended Sunday school and youth groups in his growing-up days. But he was just jumping through religious hoops. Spiritual reality for him was not found in going to church and trying to be a good person. It came in a counterfeit form as, in his teenage years, he began to drink heavily. Finally, in his early twenties, he hit bottom. He knew he needed help. He was not about to turn to the church. He had never found spiritual reality there. Instead, he joined Alcoholics Anonymous, claiming the help of his 'higher power' to live one day at a time.

Over 20 years ago, through a strange set of circumstances, he and I had lunch. I invited him to church. He bluntly informed me that he had tried that and, frankly, had not found spiritual reality. Instead, he had found it at AA. He was somewhat startled when I told him that the name of his 'higher power' is Jesus Christ, and that Jesus Christ is in the business of transforming lives. And not only does he offer forgiveness. He challenges us to a higher quality lifestyle. It's not by doing good and going to church that we are saved. We are saved by God's grace and then, through the work of the Holy Spirit, the Lord impacts how we use our time, our money, our power, and our sexuality.

My friend took the challenge to join a small group of men who met once a week for Bible study, personal sharing, and prayer. He made it clear that he was a seeker, not a believer. One year later, he asked me out for lunch. He declared, 'I am now ready to acknowledge that the name of my higher power is Jesus Christ!' The Holy Spirit has impacted his relationship with his wife and with his children. He has turned his sexuality, his money, and his power over to Jesus Christ. He is now well into 30 years of sobriety. He is not just playing church. He is trying to be like Jesus. And his wife, also now a believer in Jesus, confirms the positive change in their relationship.

There is more to the Christian life than trying to follow the example of Jesus. If you reduce the Bible to its central message, you will discover that you are created by God and loved very much by him. He has made you in his image with the capacity for moral choice. However, the Bible says that the very first two human beings took advantage of their freedom, making a decision to go against God's will. Scripture says that the entire human race is affected by the rebellion of Adam and Eve. Something has gone wrong with God's perfect creation. The Bible calls it sin and defines it as an active or passive rebellion against God. You and I are caught up in this. '... All have sinned and fall short of the glory of God' (Rom. 3:23).

Deep within each of us is a tendency to go our own way against the God who created us. That's what causes family problems. It is out of this inner rebellion against God's will that there is tension between husband and wife, parent and child. That is why you and I need to be remade into the image of God.

The Bible says that God still loves each of us, even though we are sinners. Jesus Christ took the action necessary to restore you and me to a right relationship with God. Through the miracle of God becoming a man, through the death and resurrection of Jesus Christ, you can be remade. In the process your family can have a *brand-new you.*

In order for this to happen, you must receive Jesus Christ as your Savior, allowing him to enter your life. This takes an act of the will in which you acknowledge, 'I am a sinner. I need you, God. I want your transformation of my life. I place my trust in Jesus Christ and am willing to be remade.'

If you are willing to take this step, or if you have already received Jesus Christ as your Savior, you qualify to receive his help for family living. You now have resources of power that come from outside your own personal potential. You have the presence of God's Holy Spirit. He is an energizing, enabling, spiritual power and person. You have the power of prayer in which you can bring directly to God the difficulties of everyday family living. You have the assurance of God's help. You have more than 8,000 promises in the Scriptures applicable to you as a believer in Jesus Christ – promises that are not available to those who have not accepted him as Savior. His sanctifying presence in your life makes daily, gradual transformations possible even decades after initially receiving Christ as Savior.

Jim and Marcia are their real names. They have given me permission to tell their story. Their son Doug was born into a home filled with strife. Jim was just beginning his dental practice. Marcia was going through the adjustments of her transition from competent secretary to mother and homemaker. Yes, occasionally they went to church. They tried to be good people. Somehow they couldn't get a handle on their problems. They came within an inch of separation. Wanting Doug to have a religious influence in his life, they chanced upon a little church in Key Biscayne, Florida. They brushed up against an energetic young pastor named Lane Adams who was not embarrassed to tell this sophisticated, culturally Christian couple that they needed to be born again. Jim and Marcia measured their options. Would it be worth the embarrassment to their friends and family? They made their decision, opening their lives to Christ. They were converted as individuals. They gave each other a brand-new partner.

There was only one thing wrong. Both Jim and Marcia still had the same package of problems. Jesus didn't come in and take away their difficulties. Jim continued to be a headstrong, stubborn, young professional. Marcia was still a highly independent young woman, adjusting to the confining elements of motherhood. What they both found was that Jesus Christ was willing to give them help outside of their own natural resources. The marriage was saved. They dropped their plans for separation. They were willing to go to work on their problems with the help and the strength of the Lord.

Today, almost 40 years later, Marcia tells how God helped her. Now the mother of three grown children and a participant in a healthy marriage that has had to deal with all the ups and downs couples meet over many decades, she describes those early months of Christian living. She relates two prayers that became her daily, private utterances to God after she and Jim accepted Jesus as Savior.

*Prayer one*: 'Dear Jesus, please restore my love for Jim.'
She doesn't hesitate to say that she had been questioning her love. Coming to Christ had not restored that love immediately. It took effort on her part. Day in and day out, she claimed the promises of God's Word, believing that this love could be regained. What had been deadened by the strong ego and selfishness of two people could come alive by the delicate, gracious influence of God's activity in those same two lives. Gradually, the love eased back into life for Jim and Marcia.

*Prayer two*: 'God, help me keep my big mouth shut.'
That was her biggest problem. They were two quick-witted young people with razor-sharp tongues. They had developed a highly skilled manner of doing verbal battle. Her prayer wasn't, 'Lord, help Jim to keep his mouth shut'. That's what a lot of people pray, that God will change their partner. Marcia discovered that she could ask God's control for herself. That's a powerful discovery.

We've stayed in touch with Jim and Marcia Youngblood. If you were to travel to Florida and talk with them today, you would discover that they make no pretence of a perfect marriage. There are still times when those egos get out of control and when the tensions come back. However, they will be the first to confirm that Jesus Christ can give you help outside of your own resources. Their growing, loving, communicating marriage proves his capacity to refurbish broken family relationships. Their children have been the beneficiaries of their claiming Christ's new creation.

Second, *Jesus Christ gives you a new look at your family.*
Not only do you have Christ's conversionary resources, but you have the objective promises of the Scriptures and the strength of the Holy Spirit. As a Christian, you also have the Bible that gives specific instructions relating to family living.

For example, if you are a teenager who loves Jesus Christ, you are in a position to learn what the Bible teaches about who you should marry. You are instructed not to be unequally yoked together with unbelievers. You will save yourself a lifetime of marital unhappiness if you decide, once and for all, that you will not marry an unbeliever. This is not an easy decision to make. It will have an influence on your social life. I have never yet known anyone to marry someone they haven't dated. If you consistently date nonbelievers, the chances are that you will marry a nonbeliever. You will then either have to sacrifice some of your convictions for the sake of marital oneness or you will have to go it alone within the marriage, not being able to share full spiritual comradery.

Many problems will be solved if you allow Jesus Christ to be the Lord of your social life. It may mean going without invitations to some important events. It may mean gearing your social life to church youth activities or to those of the Christian group in the high school – activities that may not be quite as appealing to you as those of the secular crowd. You do want to be mature, don't you? What is maturity? Maturity is the capacity to postpone immediate gratification for the ultimate good. By saying 'no' to certain social relationships now, you are released to a higher quality of life later on.

Anne and I do not claim to have a perfect marriage. Each of us has made our mistakes, and we have had our ups and downs along the way. But we have fewer potential problems today because we are both fellow believers in Jesus Christ. It was tough for us to say 'no' during those teenage years. Anne was 21 years old before she met me. I was 23 before I met her. There was many a doubt, many a question, many a temptation along the line. Yet we were firmly committed to going God's way. Each of us today will confirm that his way is best!

The Bible not only tells you who you can marry, it also teaches an attitude of *permanence* that is necessary to have a successful marriage. Two become one till death doth part. This 'one-flesh' concept runs diametrically opposed to society's understanding of marriage. Many people see marriage as a road to personal happiness. The Christian who takes the Bible seriously sees marriage as the way to make another person happy. All too often we Christians allow our views to be distorted by those of nonbelievers caught up in a happiness syndrome. We find ourselves disillusioned if our partner does not perform in the way that brings us ultimate happiness. Jesus said that the first shall be last and the last shall be first. That wasn't pious gibberish. That was down-to-earth psychology. If you and I gear our lives to pampering our own narcissistic, self-gratifying whims, we will be unhappy. If you are the number one person in your life, you are a miserable person. If Jesus Christ is first and your partner is second, you will find your own fulfillment to be much greater.

The Bible also helps you discover a sense of '*we-ness*' that can revolutionize your understanding of who you are. We live in a day in which so many of us are out for number one. We see our own individual happiness as the measure of how successful our family life is. That egocentric perspective is malignant in a relationship.

The Apostle Paul, in the first century, wrote these words: 'If anyone does not provide for his relatives, and especially for his immediate family, he has denied the faith and is worse than an unbeliever' (1 Tim. 5:8).

I am convinced that much of the trouble in contemporary families comes from unmitigated selfishness.

Judith Wallerstein and Sandra Blakeslee are the authors of *The Good Marriage: How and Why Love Lasts*. Wallerstein, who is known particularly for her earlier study of the long-term effects of divorce on children, decided that she needed to identify and describe happy marriages. She is engaged in a 25-year follow-up study of youngsters whose parents divorced in the early 70s when American divorce rates began to rise. A lot of these young people are saying they have never seen a single happy marriage. She declares, 'That began to scare me more and more.' One of the unintended side effects of the high divorce rate is that many young people are avoiding marriage. Yet she contends that as the stresses and demands of the workplace increase and the sense of belonging to an extended family and to a community declines, people need a happy marriage more than ever.

Wallerstein argues that marriages can maintain romance even after 20 or 30 years and that marriage benefits if each partner looks up to the other person, seeing their spouse as very special. She notes that there are several kinds of marriage. She prefers the 'romantic' marriage to the 'companionate', the 'rescue' and the 'traditional' marriage, although each of these can be happy and each offers its own challenges. She warns, though, that those in companionate marriages, who do not give enough attention to maintaining their life as a couple, can become more like brother and sister than husband and wife. Those in a traditional marriage, in which the man is the primary bread-winner and the woman devotes herself to child rearing, homemaking and providing comfort and emotional support, can still find fulfillment. But the danger here is that the couple may focus so much on their children that they find themselves distant from one another and with little in common when the children leave home. Then she notes that those who had suffered terrible abuse or neglect in childhood could still form happy and satisfying rescue marriages, designed to heal the hurts of the past. Each knows each other's story quite well and are helpful to each other. She notes that they have to give extra-special attention to not repeat destructive patterns from the past.

Wallerstein's conclusions – drawn not from a Christian perspective but from that of a secularist – bear out biblical truth about marriage. The couples she sees who are doing the best job of building healthy marriages have the ability, out of love and empathy:

'... to create what I think of as a third person in a marriage – the marriage itself, as a separate entity worth considering and fighting for. When facing problems or decisions, the couple asks not just "Is this good for me, or for you," but "How will this affect the marriage?" Many people have never created this sense of marriage as a "we-ness" worth nurturing and protecting. Marriages without such a sense are seldom strong enough to survive the trials and crises of life.'

The Bible says that you are someone very special, and God really does care for you. Your spouse is someone very special, and God really does care for him or her. He doesn't expect you to be perfect or your spouse to be perfect. He quietly and calmly welcomes you to his family and declares your worth and the worth of everyone you know. You, your partner, your children are a family – not just an assorted group of individuals. This 'we-ness' is so important. God's guidance is firm and loving. There is much that his Word tells you about how to have a healthy relationship with him and with each other that is as up-do-date as the most-recent psychological and sociological textbook.

Third, *Jesus Christ helps you admit when you are wrong.*
As a Christian, you are able to admit that you are a sinner. When you have bent your knee to God, it is much easier to bend your knee to another human being. When you confess to God and have been accepted by him, you find it much easier to confess your faults to those with whom you live so closely. When you can bend your knee to God and say, 'I am sorry,' your ego can survive the devastating blow of having to go to your partner and say, 'I am sorry.' Anne and I have had to work at this.

By nature, I tend to be a defensive person. I really try to do things the right way.

Obviously, I fail. I am particularly defensive when Anne points out some imperfection, inconsistency or major blemish in my life. I have all kinds of excuses, the biggest being, 'I am really trying to do things right.' As I try daily to honestly confess my sins to God, I become increasingly aware not only of my need for his forgiveness but also of my need to ask for Anne's forgiveness. The three hardest words in the English language to say are, 'I was wrong.' However, they are also three of the most liberating words when I have the guts to nondefensively admit my mistake or my wrong attitude. And the positive change that comes over Anne is amazing.

I am happy to report that we are making headway in our relationship when it comes to apologizing to each other.

I have learned, through the years, the importance of not just apologizing to my wife but also apologizing to my children.

One day when our children were small, Anne and I had some harsh words with each other. I had been overbearing. I had been unkind. In normal circumstances, we would slip away to the bedroom, have a few moments of prayer together, give each other a big hug and kiss and find that release which comes from saying, 'I am sorry.' I'll admit that sometimes, when feelings were stuffed under the surface and even when we had said we were sorry to each other, a residue would build up that could leak around the edges in resentment and misunderstanding. We had to go deeper than simply saying, 'I am sorry.'

On this particular occasion, I saw that one of our daughters, who was then three years old, was watching and listening as Anne and I came to the end of our verbal skirmish. Suddenly it dawned on me that these little ears and eyes were taking in some data that was not good. Instead of going to the bedroom with Anne, I turned to her and said, 'Daddy has been a bad boy. Daddy needs a spanking, doesn't he?' Little Suzanne's eyes became as big as saucers. Her shocked expression quickly changed to an ear-to-ear smile so big you would have thought she had a coat hangar caught in her mouth. Her response was, 'Daddy, naughty too?!'

What she was saying was that to her mind she was the naughty one in our family. Mommy and Daddy never admitted that they were wrong. Sure she saw them do things that were wrong. For the first time, her perspective shifted as we honestly acknowledged what we had done wrong. As tough as it may be to do, begin to admit to your children when you are wrong. You know you are wrong. They know you are wrong. Why not admit it?

This sets you up for those adult years ahead when these little ones, who initially stand in awe of us, ultimately come to their own sense of autonomy and stake their individuality apart from us. If we ever want to be friends with them, we need to face the fact that we will need to be engaged in a healthy exchange of ideas, opinions and sometimes even painful conduct in which, 'I am sorry. Please forgive me,' is the request that will help cut through the defensiveness of our adult-adult relationships.

The same Suzanne, some 20 years later, was fighting a losing battle with Hodgkin's Disease. Two months before she died, she wrote me a letter. In that letter she confronted me honestly, firmly, lovingly, with some actions and attitudes she observed in my life that she thought needed to be changed. As painful as it was to confront those realities, a pattern had been established that gave her the freedom to write that letter. With God's help, it gave me the freedom to respond, not in my typical defensiveness but in genuine repentance before God, Suzanne, and the rest of the family. It wasn't easy to say, 'I was wrong.' Sometimes we need to say it.

Fourth, *Jesus Christ enables you to back up a family member when they are wrong.*
Once you understand your own imperfection and sinful nature and can admit your own faults, you are much more sympathetic to the faults of others. You know who you are. You know who they are. You can back them up in their failure, even as they back you up in yours.

I remember years ago, when I lived in Key Biscayne, that an FBI agent spoke to our Kiwanis Club in downtown Miami. He gave a talk on drug abuse. It was one of those tough law-and-order addresses. At the end of his talk, he said, 'If I ever catch my son smoking marijuana or using drugs of any kind, I will grab him by the scruff of his neck, shake him until his teeth rattle, point my finger in his face and say, "You are not my son!"' Do you know what we did? We, members of the largest Kiwanis Club in the world, unanimously jumped to our feet and gave him a standing ovation. That was great. We loved that tough talk on law and order. That's the way to handle the drug problem!

As I walked out of that hotel ballroom, my heart sank. No, that isn't the way to handle a son caught up in drugs. In fact, it would probably be the best way to cause him to get involved since it would communicate the insecurity of, 'I'm accepted only if I'm perfect.'

I thought of my own dad. I must have been ten or eleven. I had thrown a rock at a friend. It missed him but went through the front window of the neighbor's house a block and a half away from our Arlington, Massachusetts, home. The neighbor apparently recognized my tail end as I disappeared around the corner. Although I hid in the basement, it wasn't long before the front door bell rang. My father went to the door. The neighbor said, 'I think your Johnny just threw a rock through my window.' What was my dad's response? 'Oh, no, Johnny is the preacher's son. He wouldn't do a thing like that.' Not at all. He found me in the basement. He brought me up and asked me in front of the neighbor, 'Did you break the window?' I had to admit it. Did he open his wallet and take out a ten-dollar bill, saying, 'Here. Go get the window fixed'? No, he didn't. He said, 'Johnny and I will take care of fixing that window.'

Together we went to the hardware store. Dad bought a window pane, putty and the necessary tools. We drove to the neighbor's house. There, the local preacher spent a couple of hours – with his son by his side – fixing that window. I want to tell you something. I never threw another rock that broke another window. In fact, from that time on, I didn't do as many things wrong as I could have done. Why? Because my dad stood by me when I was wrong. I felt the security of his love, his care.

I didn't want ever to embarrass him again. Jesus Christ enables you to stand by those you love when they are wrong.

Jesus Christ doesn't take away your problems. He helps you handle them, giving you outside resources. He gives you a responsible outlook on family living, and the ability to admit it when you are wrong and stand by those you love when they are wrong. Are you accepting what he wants you to do for your family? At the very deepest level, all this practical talk about relationship falls short if we have not confronted our own need of Christ's forgiveness for our failures to be all he created us to be. 1 John 1:8-9 reads:

> If we claim to be without sin, we deceive ourselves and the truth is not in us. If we confess our sins, he is faithful and just and will forgive us our sins and purify us from all unrighteousness.

It's not always easy to face up to the fact we are sinners and need God's forgiveness. When we do, we are much better able to live with ourselves and those significant others whom God has entrusted to us, claiming his help outside of our own resources and his new look at our family relationships.

CHAPTER 4

# WHY WORK SHOULD BE YOUR FOURTH PRIORITY

*If anyone does not provide for his relatives, and especially for his immediate family, he has denied the faith and is worse than an unbeliever*

1 Timothy 5:8

You and I have the privilege and the responsibility of providing for the material needs of our families.

The Apostle Paul wrote to the young pastor Timothy, 'If anyone does not provide for his relatives, and especially for his immediate family, he has denied the faith and is worse than an unbeliever' (1 Tim. 5:8).

The first time I ever seriously confronted that verse was when I saw it printed on the stationery of what then was called the Presbyterian Ministers' Fund Life Insurance Company, the oldest life insurance company in the United States. At that time it insured only ministers and their immediate families. What a great sales pitch for buying life insurance! In fact, I was so impressed by that verse that I looked it up in the Bible just to be sure it was there.

Economic considerations are biblically significant. Careful perusal of the Scriptures alerts us not to be so heavenly minded that we are of no earthly good. Things are important. Christianity does not minimize material matters. Jesus Christ made constant reference to God's material provision. Both the Old and New Testament give historical account of how God has taken care of his own.

Unfortunately, extremists have led people in false directions. On the one hand history portrays those who are hedonists,

pampering every little sensual appetite and devoting their primary energies to material whims. At the other extreme there are
the ascetics who make a religious appeal to self-denial. There
is a biblical call to discipline. This must not be confused with
a depreciation of God-given physical gifts. Hedonism on one
extreme and asceticism on the other are perversions of how
God created us to live.

The Bible outlines a theology of creation. God has created
all that is in the world. Our physical presence is important. As
we dedicate our energies to spiritual growth, we must realize
that this is to be carried out in this physical world within our
human body. As believers in Christ, we live in a constant tension to succumb to being either overly or underly concerned
with material matters. The Bible has a lot more to say about our
physical and economic existence than we may realize. Within
this context, let me raise seven significant questions relative to
meeting your family's material needs.

Question one: *Are you working hard?*
There is no place for a lazy Christian. God instituted a work
ethic. He did it even in the most idyllic setting, the Garden of
Eden. Prior to the fall of Adam and Eve in sin, he gave them
responsibility to take care of his creation in very practical
ways.

What kind of a work ethic do you have? We are talking
about your daily, down-to-earth routine.

New Englander Fulton Rindge was a sage textile executive.
He commented about a lazy associate, saying, 'If he worked half
as hard at doing something productive as he does at trying to
avoid work, he would be a millionaire!' Some people are just
plain lazy. They work hard in an endeavor to avoid work. How
about you?

While in Florida for six years, from 1968 through 1973, I observed an interesting phenomenon. I observed many hard-working northern businessmen as they vacationed in Florida. They
would tell me how they couldn't wait to retire. With jealous

eyes, some gazed at colleagues fortunate enough to take early retirement. I then watched some of these men move south. They arrived in their mid-sixties, enthusiastic about their newfound opportunity to play golf seven days a week. A strange thing happened. Unless they had developed a productive *avocation* – something that made a contribution beyond play – many of these men shriveled up into retrospective living. They were addicted to the past. In their non-retirement vacations they would fantasize about the time when they could play golf every day. Now many a retired person's conversation in a country club locker room was loaded with the reminiscences of the good old life at work. Double martinis lubricated melancholy musings of better days back on the job.

What could be better than a life of full-time play? I will tell you what – a good, hard life of productive work! I have observed the same phenomenon since coming to Southern California in 1978. There are persons who move down to Newport Beach from Los Angeles, thrilled to be retired, who simply waste away in their retirement years, bored with life. There are others who refuse to retire from life, knowing that there are just so many rounds of golf one can play and just so many trips one can take. We were created to be a productive person, even in our retirement.

What a joy it has been to discover occasional retirees who develop their lifelong hobby into creative work.

Claude Ruch was one of these. Retired from Field Enterprises in Chicago, he found plenty of time for watercolor painting. Not only that. He started teaching art classes. Along with dedicated work for Jesus Christ in his church, he made a positive contribution working hard in his retirement. How different is his story from that of my friend Bill, the retired insurance agent from another northern city, who soon died from the boredom of golf and alcoholic over-indulgence.

I have a friend in his early fifties. He is the heir to one of the nation's largest fortunes. He draws on a trust account that provides all the money he needs to support his family in a luxurious lifestyle. Talk about restlessness. He wants to work. But he doesn't have to. So he dabbles at this job and then that job. Occasionally he experiences some sense of accomplishment. However, freed from the necessity of having to get along with people just to put bread on the table, he has developed a pattern of insulting his business associates, dramatically resigning, walking away from his job when the going gets tough.

Are you yearning for retirement? Are you jealous of that friend who doesn't have to work? The Bible clearly teaches that work is a God-given responsibility and privilege. The fall of Adam and Eve was followed by the curse of God which said, 'By the sweat of your brow you will eat your food until you return to the ground, since from it you were taken; for dust you are and to dust you will return' (Gen. 3:19).

Romans 12:11 urges Christians to not be slothful in business. You and I are fulfilled in our work. We try to take so many shortcuts. Your job is both your curse and your blessing. It is difficult. Yet there are God-given rewards. You are called to help your marriage partner if you are married. Together you have the responsibility to provide for yourself and your family. You are to help each other.

We need to be particularly sensitive to single persons, especially single mothers who, with great nobility, are endeavoring to provide for their children. We need to encourage them in this. How sad it is to see a society that deserts its women, forcing them to be wards of the state. As family members, we are to do all we can to help those who, for whatever reason, need help.

I ask the question: Are you working hard? You should be, with a strong sense of vocation. If you are able to work, thank God. God has called you and me to good, hard labor!

Question two: *What are your priorities?*
One of the most rewarding pastoral experiences is to observe men and women sincerely endeavoring to sort out competing priorities in lifestyles. How exciting it is to discover someone in

mid-career who is willing to admit that his life is out of kilter, who is willing to reorganize, reprioritize so that first things will be first.

Even as the Bible stresses the importance of good, hard work, it also calls you to periodically reanalyze your priorities.

One of my mentors in ministry was Dr. Richard C. Halverson who pastored the Fourth Presbyterian Church in Washington and then for many years was the Chaplain of the United States Senate. Dr. Halverson died in 1995.

As I went back to Washington to attend his memorial service, I was reminded that he was the first person to confront me with this radical, revolutionary concept of reprioritizing one's life. Dr. Halverson would say, 'First comes your commitment to Jesus Christ; second your commitment to your marriage partner; third, your commitment to your children; and fourth, your commitment to your work.'

I believe this. I work at this prioritization, not always as successfully as I would idealize.

You say, 'How in the world can you square that up – putting your career fourth – with the importance of work? It seems as if work is being lowered instead of raised in its importance.' In fact, the opposite is true. If you put Jesus Christ first, your partner second, your children third, and your work fourth, ultimately, you will make a much greater contribution in your job.

You've seen it happen time after time. A man is career oriented. Work is everything. Spiritual matters are neglected. The wife and children are not taken seriously. For ten or fifteen years, he sprints ahead in his profession. Seven days a week he plows his energies into being successful. He makes it to the top only to find out he no longer knows his God, his wife or his children.

I know one man, a lawyer, who has risen to the very top of his profession. Night after night he burned the midnight oil at his office. He has literally run through two wives with his inattention and, right now, is oblivious to the fact he is wrecking a third marriage. His wife is starved for relationship.

We ministers can be as prone to this as anyone else. Every time I start burning the candle at both ends, robbing time from Anne and the girls, I am reminded of one of the most accomplished preachers in America. He is now dead. Forty years ago he was at the top of his career. His daughter, then in her early twenties, told me, 'Everybody else seems to know my dad. But I don't. And he doesn't know me. He's driven by his career!' I can still see that delicate blend of bitterness and sadness that marked her countenance as she spoke.

Now we are seeing the same phenomenon with women who are putting their careers ahead of their marriage partners and their children.

What a price they ultimately pay!

I remember the night Anne and I met with the pastoral nominating committee of the First Presbyterian Church of Pittsburgh where we served for five years in the 1970s. They asked me about my priorities. I outlined this 'Christ/wife/children/work' order. I can still remember that all nine sets of eyebrows raised in unison. Lips pursed as nine minds pondered. This was Pittsburgh in the early 1970s. Pittsburgh, a steel town, was proud of its work ethic. It was known for tolerating no nonsense when it came to hard work. There they were, individually musing on what I had said. Then quick sideways glances were made to each other as, in unison, smiles came over their faces, authenticating the validity of this set of priorities.

This is particularly tough in our contemporary environment where so many husbands and wives either need to work or think they need to work. Is it possible that some people have no idea how to sacrifice anymore? Do some put themselves in the position of 'needing' two salaries, to the detriment of their kids?

My wife Anne has pointed out an interesting aspect to this prioritization. She has observed that we have God in Jesus Christ for eternity. Hopefully we have our spouse for life. We have our children until we encourage them to walk away from us as adults and then, hopefully, they rediscover us as friends. And we have our jobs for an indefinite time. It used to be that a person could go with a company and expect to stay with that firm until they retired with their gold watch and their pension at age 65. That's no longer the case. People who put Jesus Christ first, spouse second, children third, and work fourth are people who will ultimately make a much greater vocational contribution to society. Because their life is balanced, there is a much smaller chance that society will have to employ one more social worker to tidy up the mess they have made out of their domestic life. This person is not as apt to be a drain on company resources when they break down physically or emotionally from truncated living. They have balance. They are plugged into God, family and work with a wholeness of living that lets them engage their work creatively.

Yes, you and I are to work hard. But at the same time, you and I better take a look at our priorities. Let me ask you this question: Are your priorities in line?

I remember being at a Christmas party. There had been a happy hour preceding the dinner. I had had nothing to drink stronger than coffee. Therefore, fully sober, I was, on this occasion as on others, confronted with a situation that would be semi-hilarious if it had not been so tragic. A man in his early seventies, whom I had never seen before, stepped up to me, poked me in the stomach, and, in a voice which clearly betrayed his recent familiarity with the fruit of the vine, said, 'Hey, Reverend, I've got something to tell you. I've made quite a bit of money in my life. In fact, I'm a millionaire several times over. I've given my kids everything. But you know something? Next to my wife here, there is only one other person in the world who loves me. That's my dog. My kids hate me! So my wife and I have taken care of them. Tell the Reverend what we've done, Honey.' His wife said, 'No. You tell him.' Before she had time to finish, he was back into his story without ever stopping to take a breath. 'Last week we rewrote our will. We are willing our home, our Lincoln Continental, and the services of our chauffeur and all that it takes to keep up our home, our car, our chauffeur – to our dog.'

This man obviously had failed to realize a proper set of priorities. He was hurting. That was clear. He had succeeded in making material provision for his own. In the process, he had neglected certain spiritual and emotional needs, totally alienating his children and perhaps even his wife.

Are you concentrating too much on making material provision to the neglect of spiritual and emotional priorities?

Question three: *What kind of model are you?*
People learn from models. Much of what you do has been learned from watching other persons. If you have been fortunate enough to study a successful businessperson, you have probably found yourself copying that person's methods and even lifestyle. Right now, someone is watching you and perhaps even copying you. You teach your children more by your performance than by what you tell them. They adopt your attitudes. They learn from you what money is. They learn from you how to make it. They learn from you how to spend it.

I remember being at my daughter Carla's first Parents' Day Weekend at Stanford University back in 1988. The dean of the university told us how many parents were afraid that their children would become socialists during their years at Stanford. She observed, 'Don't worry. They may shake you up with some radical thoughts when they come home on vacation, but it's amazing how quickly they revert to the laissez-faire capitalistic ideas with which you've raised them once they graduate and get into the marketplace themselves.' Let me ask you some questions about how you model for others in terms of material wealth.

What are you modeling in terms of the way you handle debt? We all know that some debt is essential for purchasing a home and running a business. But I am astounded at the reports I read about credit card abuse. I am, with greater frequency, counseling persons who have found the unyielding reality of high-rate, compounding interest working against them as their wants – put on a credit card – drastically exceeded their capacity to pay for those purchases. I know it's very easy to become addicted to this plastic credit. There are companies out there determined to addict you. I was astounded to observe my daughter Janet, when a sophomore in college, start receiving credit cards through the mail, promising the first several months at no interest. That's seductive.

Do those significant others in your life know that your commitment to Jesus Christ is so strong that you tithe, giving 10 percent before taxes to the work of Jesus Christ? If so, they will respect the seriousness of your commitment, being more apt to listen to your words. If they choose never to tithe, there will always be that haunting sense of remembering that Mom and Dad put their money where their profession of faith was. They will know the authenticity of the love of Christ in this crass, commercial world in which increasingly people are declaring, 'We can't possibly afford to tithe'.

Do your loved ones see you save, putting aside a percentage of your income for future emergencies? Do they have that kind of a model? Are they seeing you manage your money with an eye to providing for the future?

My friends Dick and Ruth Nelson recently returned from visiting their children and grandchildren in Illinois. They told of the Willow Creek Church, pastored by Bill Hybels, where an all-day seminar was given to teach young couples how to handle their money. The whole thesis was that the starting point is putting 10 percent off the top, the tithe, into the work of Jesus Christ. Then the next 10 percent is taken and put away in savings. If you can't do that, then you have to analyze what is out of kilter in the rest of your life. You may have to drastically alter your lifestyle. That may involve getting rid of that extra car, which may not be a painless process. But even as businesses downsize, families may need to do some of that also. What is your attitude toward the poor? What do your children see in you?

When we talk about making material provision for our families, we are not just talking about money. This involves our habits of life.

Do you exercise? Do you watch your diet? Are you a good steward of the physical resources God has given to you? Your children and grandchildren are looking to you for a model. Do you smoke? Just a moment. This preacher is beginning to meddle, isn't he?

Some years ago I read about a hot financial tip for young people describing a sure-fire way to boost their net worth substantially at no risk at all, and of a fat nest egg at retirement. This was back in the early seventies. The suggestion was simply to stop smoking and invest the money saved. Some physicians had figured out how much it would cost the average person to smoke one pack of cigarettes a day for 40 years and what that amount would yield at eight percent interest compounded monthly. The total then was $56,000. That was before galloping inflation when a pack of cigarettes cost a lot less. The savings for a teenager today would be considerably larger than that. And you might just save something else – your life. That same article said that the chances of developing lung cancer are 20 times greater for cigarette smokers than for nonsmokers. This footnote was added: 'The primary reason for youngsters taking up the smoking habit is not magazine advertising, movies, or smoking friends. It is smoking by parents....'

Our children watch us closely. Our good habits and our bad habits shape them. Some of these habits have horrendous implications. Fortunately, today, many have stopped smoking. But there are other negative habits that model destructive patterns for our loved ones.

I am astonished every time I realize that more people are killed in auto accidents caused by drunken drivers here in the United States each year than the total number of American soldiers killed during the entire Vietnam War. Think of the additional disruption to family stability caused by alcohol abuse plus the physical destruction on the human body and the high economic cost of lost work hours. Talk about the negative impact of drugs. Alcoholic beverages are a legal drug destroying our society. Granted, the Bible doesn't prohibit moderate consumption. But it does speak strongly about drunkenness, and all of us know what tragic circumstances can emerge from intended moderation that goes out of control.

I was reminded this week of how important we are as models. Candy Baylis, who's in charge of our church's preschool, sent me a memo about a little boy in the program. It told how often he lies and how destructive his behavior has been. The other day he smashed the watch of one of our girls. He stomped on it until it was broken into little bits. But he wouldn't face up to what he had done. One of our teachers worked with him for the longest time, trying to help him know that God does not like lying. It makes him sad. After much conversation, he admitted that he had smashed the watch. Later his teacher came across an envelope labeled, 'To God.' Inside it was this letter:

> Dear God, I love you. I am sorry for hitting and being mean. Please help me to be a good boy. Love....

Someone is doing a good job of modeling.

Are you a good model of stewardship, showing how best to live your life?

Question four: *Are you prepared for tough times?*
In all our stress on providing for our own, we have to face the fact that there are times of economic reversal. Seldom does a family get through life without economic strains. Reversal is a part of life. If there is a pattern of good, hard work, the tough times don't permanently hurt. In fact, they help pull the family together and teach the children lessons they could learn no other way.

During my first 14 years of life my father pastored a small church in Cambridge, Massachusetts. During the 1940s he sold his car to pay the church's fuel bill. For the better part of a year he rode his bike or took the bus to work. Did that permanently mar my life? Absolutely not! Our family had bad times and good times, financially. I probably learned more about money and sincerity of purpose in the bad times than in the good. I had my paper routes. I worked as a caddy. I was encouraged to be an entrepreneur as I worked my way through high school, college, and seminary. The tough times were good for me.

My sister Miriam went through a time of comparative ease during her last couple of years of high school and her first year in college. Then my mother and father had some reversals. My sister had the humbling experience of renting out her services to do housework in homes and for the mothers of some of her closest friends. That was the making of my sister. In a spiritual, personal way, hardship builds character.

Tough times pull a family together. I know one family in which the father has been laid off from his local employment. Each day he drives 60 miles one way just to have work. You can see the family pulling together during this time of difficulty.

If you are diligent in your work, God's blessing is with you. He rewards your faithfulness, even if you never make a lot of money or if you go through times of deep financial discouragement.

Question five: *What is your attitude toward your partner's work?*
Is it one of appreciation? Do you stop to think what your spouse is doing for you? It is so important to express appreciation. You can destroy by your complaints and comparisons. I know a woman who has tunnel vision when it comes to her husband. They strained themselves to buy a home a bit beyond their means. It's a beautiful home in a lovely suburb. Her husband makes pretty good money. But by buying the home she wanted, the monthly payments and taxes have kept her from being able to match the economic lifestyle of her neighbors. They can't afford to join the proper clubs or take the best vacations. She constantly nags her husband about his failure to provide. He has provided. She lacks appreciation. Her ideals are too high. She doesn't realize that she is the envy of some whose husbands don't do quite as well. In the process, she is missing an enormous blessing of God upon her life. She is like a kid in a

candy store. Her eyes are too big. Her nickel doesn't go as far as she wants it to go.

You can get so caught up in your own work that you forget the importance of what your partner does. Some of us men are guilty of this. A wife works hard. Just imagine if you had to prepare those meals for your family, wash the dishes, clean the house, do the laundry, iron your own shirts, take care of the kids. Those jobs take seven days a week. Now it's all the more complicated if your wife also has a job outside of the home. She needs all the more help and understanding. Do you ever express your appreciation? Do you ever pitch in and help? What's your attitude toward your partner's work?

Question six: *What are you doing for your parents?*
Are you taking care of those who expended so much energy in taking care of you? That's why Paul addresses this matter of widows and the care for them by their children and grandchildren.

When Paul writes about providing for our relatives, he specifically mentions widows who have lost their means of support. Some of these women were made widows by the death of their husband. Others in the New Testament context had become widows for the sake of Jesus Christ. Coming to personal faith in Jesus Christ had been costly for them. They were not to divorce their nonbelieving husbands, but their pagan spouses deserted many of these early converted women. Paul was urging nuclear families to take care of mothers and grandmothers who were incapable of supporting themselves. He wrote:

> Give proper recognition to those widows who are really in need. But if a widow has children or grandchildren, these should learn first of all to put their religion into practice by caring for their own family and so repaying their parents and grandparents, for this is pleasing to God (1 Tim. 5:3-4).

Charity begins at home. E. K. Simpson said, 'A religious profession which falls below the standard of duty recognized by the world is a wretched fraud.' Secular writers have empha-sized our responsibilities toward our parents to make provision for them. Philo wrote, 'When old storks become unable to fly, they remain in their nests and are fed by their children, who go to endless exertions to provide their food because of their piety.' He noted that even the animal creation acknowledges its obligation to aged parents. How much more should we as Christian men and women.

I appreciate how difficult it is to know what to do with ag-ing parents. We were once their children. Now they've become ours. What we do for them becomes a model for what ours will do for us. In turn, elderly parents have a responsibility to respect and adapt to their child's provision. Many parents have caused themselves to be pushed out of a loving home by forgetting that they are no longer responsible for the leadership role. One must take a backseat to the leadership of one's children.

What higher symbol of Christian grace can be seen today than children who are making provision for their elderly par-ents? What are you doing for yours?

Question seven: *What are you doing with your discretionary time?* Are you doing things for other people? Are you allowing your heart to be broken by the things that break the heart of God?

I've had to struggle with this. Everything within me wanted to say 'no' to being Chairman of the Board of World Vision U.S. I had already given nine years of my time to serving on that board with its requirements of attending four meetings per year and occasionally traveling to international project sites. Being the Chair of the Board would mean the addition of serving on the International Board and its Executive Committee. It would demand at least two international trips per year. And it would be tough to explain to some of my church members why I would have to miss some activities due to that travel. If I would say 'no', I would have more time for personal pursuits.

So, when in 1995 this challenge came my way, I had to prayerfully determine what God would have me do. This would involve two three-year terms, back to back, taking me through the year 2001. Well, now it's very clear that my 'yes' was the right answer. God, through His Holy Spirit, communicated both to me and our church leaders that this extra time commitment would be worth it. And those few extra days every year, taken from my vacation and study leave, have been such a rewarding investment as I've been able to join with others in serving the poorest of the poor in over 100 countries. My mind and heart come alive with a collage of pictures and grateful faces in places as varying as Vietnam, Brazil, Bosnia, Uganda, Lebanon, and China. This is my servant ministry.

What is yours? You have some discretionary time. How creative are you in the use of it? You are especially gifted by God. You have unique capacities to encourage persons in your family, your church, work, in your social circle, and even the somewhat disadvantaged in the larger community.

Perhaps you are already working hard, prioritizing wisely, modeling well, preparing for tough times, valuing your part-ner's work, giving attention to your parents to the extent you don't feel you have any discretionary time. You are running so hard and so fast to meet the material needs of your nuclear and extended family that the notion of servant ministry to those beyond that circle seems impossible.

Whatever your circumstances, you and I, at least, can be alert to the possibility of the task within a task. We can maximize every situation in which we find ourselves by seeing ourselves as being deployed by God to do not only the job assigned by others but simultaneously, in addition, a stealth job assigned by God.

For 30 years, the late Dr. David Hubbard was the president of Fuller Theological Seminary. On one occasion, I heard him pay tribute to the three most influential people in his life. One that stands out the most was a junior high school teacher who one day challenged him in private, 'David, are you going to waste the rest of your life reading those science fiction novels? You have a lot more potential than that. Let me make a deal with you.

If you read them, I'll buy you some first-class books that will really develop your mind.' He took her up on this. She bought him a book. He read it and reported back. Then she bought him another book. He read it and reported back. A friendship grew. This continued over many months. She, as every teacher, was overworked and underpaid. She came to the end of each day exhausted from the routine which was compounded by the disciplinary problems. Each night she had papers to read and tests to grade. How easy it would have been with the last bell to have made whatever preparations were necessary for the next day and to have closed the books, packed up her briefcase and headed home. Instead, she saw the privilege, a task within a task, and the opportunity to help shape a young life.

Only God knows how many other young people she helped in similar ways. What we do know is that she discovered and unleashed tremendous intellectual and spiritual gifts of a man who was one of the most innovative shapers of American theological thought and education. You and I can learn from her, deploying ourselves in servant ministries to others in an investment that will bear dividends far beyond our own lifespan. What a tremendous privilege and responsibility we have of meeting the material needs of both our nuclear and extended families and beyond!

# CHAPTER 5
## HOW TO KEEP YOUR FAMILY EMOTIONALLY HEALTHY

*If anyone does not provide for his relatives, and especially for his immediate family, he has denied the faith and is worse than an unbeliever*

1 Timothy 5:8

One of the most articulate psychiatrists in the United States is Dr. Armand Nicholi of Harvard University. In addition, he is a devout believer in Jesus Christ. Dr. Nicholi did extensive research into the campus uprisings of the late 1960s and early 1970s, probing deep into the causes of student rebellion. He has continually updated his research. He has concluded that the emotional responses of today's students and growing adult population are rooted in their early home life.

I believe that you will find Dr. Nicholi's emotional profile of some modern youth helpful in increasing your understanding.

One finds that many youth come from homes in which the family unit has virtually disintegrated. Uninvolved and absent parents, especially the father, give rise to repeated feelings of rejection and resentment.

The time demands on a highly successful father, or even on the many less successful fathers holding two jobs, result in homes virtually without paternal figures. In addition, the hours that a mother spends at home and the quality of relationship between mother and child continue to decline. When the parents do stay home, the television set and other electronic gadgets continually interfere with meaningful personal relationship.

In addition, the failure to set limits intensifies feelings within the child that the parent is uninvolved and uncaring, and leaves a residue of poor impulse control and an inability to delay gratification. The tendency to punish by withdrawal of attention and affection merely adds to the sense of being unacknowledged and rejected.

Finally, in many of the more affluent homes, parents send the child away to boarding school, adding to the long series of traumatic experiences of rejection.

In short, the particular orientation of modern society produces fragmented families, with material values superceding ethical and spiritual values and with parents confused as to limits and basic priorities. This may be related to why many of the young reject not only the materialism of our society, but the entire free enterprise system as well.

Out of this background comes the specific emotional conflicts that trouble young people today. Rejection inevitably gives rise to resentment and anger. The suspiciousness and intense anger with authority – always present to some degree in this age group – has now become considerably more intense, considerably closer to the surface, and considerably more difficult to control. Secondly, clinical problems reflect not excessive control and inhibition as in the past, but rather an inability to control impulses and to delay gratification. Thirdly, and most important of all, today's youth possess a peculiarly intense sensitivity to remote, invisible, and unresponsive authority – a direct result of early experiences with remote, unresponsive, and emotionally uninvolved (and often absent) parents.

I share this lengthy quote from Dr. Nicholi, written originally in the environment of the upheavals of the late 1960s and 1970s, only to underline the essential need of developing a healthy emotional climate in your home. Since the time he wrote these words, campus unrest has quieted down some, but the estrangement of the 'Boomer', 'Buster', and 'Generation X' generations from authority figures and institutions makes it just as relevant today.

1 Timothy 5:8 reads: 'If anyone does not provide for his relatives, and especially for his immediate family, he has denied the faith and is worse than an unbeliever.'

When the Bible instructs us to provide for our own, this not only means, as we have already seen, that we should make spiritual and material provision. I am convinced that it also necessitates us making careful *emotional* provision for our families.

Each of us has some very basic emotional needs. Let's take a look at four of the most basic that you and I and the members of our families have.

First, you need *intimate response*

That's a basic emotional necessity for everyone. It involves tenderness, sensitivity, and appreciation of the special nature of your loved one. Isn't it amazing how we move through life insensitive to the other person's need for intimate response? I've noted my own weakness at this point. Long days are spent helping people with their problems. We pastors make every effort to understand and be sensitive. In the process, I find myself driving home, sometimes late at night, exhausted after a day that began with a 7 a.m. meeting and concluded with a church committee meeting and a post-meeting discussion in the parking lot that lasted until 11 p.m. With tenderness, I try to relate with other men's wives and other men's children, encouraging them to a wholeness in Christ. Then I return home to my own wife and family, tired and not always as sensitive to them and their needs as I should be.

I remember back to my younger years as the father of young daughters in the early 1970s. One day I returned home from the office, worn out and irritable. I pulled into the driveway. Our daughters seem to attract like magnets everyone's cast-off toy vehicles. They were not content to play with one at a time. No afternoon of enjoyment was complete without wheeling all of these bikes, wagons, and animals on wheels into a carefully arranged state of disarray in the middle of our driveway. Time after time, I would pompously and chauvinistically instruct

Anne to make certain that the kids put their toys away before I came home from work. Time after time, these instructions went unheeded. By the time I got out of the car and wheeled six or seven of these vehicles into the garage, I found all of the anxieties and pressures of the day building up within me, causing an emotional response toward Anne and the children that was less than pleasant. Of course, that didn't stimulate the best response on their part either!

Fortunately, although Anne herself is not always perfect, I have a wife who works at meeting my emotional needs. I remember coming in one night all steamed up over the fact that the toys once again had not been put back in their places. I swept through the front door, a big balloon inflated with anger and frustration. Anne, busy in the kitchen, sensed my mood as I began my recital of complaints. Instead of returning a similar list of things that had gone wrong in her day, she looked at me, smiled, pursed her lips and blew me a light kiss. My big balloon full of self-important hot air was deflated. Her intimate response to both the valid and invalid aspects of my frustration brought me into a brand-new world of peace with myself and with the ones I love most.

Sometimes the harshest and most belligerent attitudes expressed by family members are coverups of their own weakness, vulnerability, or personal need. Your sensitivity, your tenderness, your love can release your loved ones to joy and peace as you are aware of their need for intimate response.

Second, you need *adventure*
Your loved ones have a need for adventure. No life is emotionally whole if there is not a sense of expectancy.

Remember your first business deal. You were working your way through school selling magazines. You were paid by commission. How excited you were with the first $20 you earned! Or perhaps it was your first day in the office on a new job. Remember the enthusiasm with which you arranged and rearranged your papers and settled in behind your new desk? It was probably a modest salary. To you it was a great adventure.

Remember that love letter which didn't come? You went out and said, 'Mr. Mailman, I am sure there is one more letter in your bag.' He looked and said, 'No, I don't believe there is.' 'But there has to be!' you responded, expecting some word from your loved one. You went through this for the next three days until finally the letter arrived. I feel confident that you have received many letters in your day. But none, I believe, was ever quite as exciting as the one you expected which didn't come, which made you all the more eager for the day when it finally arrived.

I know that some of us have settled into bland living. There is no enthusiasm. There is no excitement. There is no joy. Every day has its routine. Even if you can survive on emotional K-rations day in and day out, your partner, your children, your parents need adventure. Are you doing anything to make your family's life more exciting? Are you planning adventure?

Third, you need *security*
That's why Linus holds so tightly to his blanket. That's why your toddlers have theirs. A three-year-old drags that blanket everywhere he goes. It gets dirty and smelly. That doesn't make any difference to him. You try to keep it clean. I remember one night when one of our girls was three years old. We tucked her into bed. Suddenly we heard howls of anguish. Fearful, we rushed to her bedroom only to find that she wanted her 'blankey'. We ransacked the house, finally delivering to her this intimate symbol of security.

We are amused by a youngster's dependence. You have the same needs. Your security blanket may be your job and some of the fringe benefits that go with it. It may be your club member-ship or the sense of security and bigness you get from sitting behind the wheel of your late-model, luxury automobile. Your security may be in clothing fashions – having the proper width of tie, lapel or length of skirt. Your security may come from being attached to the 'right' church. Or it can be derived authentically from a personal relationship with God in Jesus Christ. Security is important. You can provide security for those you love. I am convinced that if our security needs are not being met by another person – whether a human being, the Person of God, or some combination of both – we will tend to latch onto material objects so as to try and find some degree of security.

Fourth, you need *recognition*
You and I need to be singled out as special!

I used to be a member of the downtown Miami Kiwanis Club. We prided ourselves on being the largest club in Kiwanis International. Every year we played a golf tournament with the Miami Rotary Club. The afternoon of golf was great sport. The most fun was the evening banquet. The most interesting part of the evening banquet was the time of recognition. Awards were given. You would imagine that the best golfer would receive an award and that the winning team would be given the traditional 'gold-plated out-house' trophy. That was just the beginning. There was an award for the worst golfer. There was one for the oldest, the best dressed, and the worst dressed. On and on this went until, finally, there was a grab bag with names for gifts to be presented to anyone whose name was drawn. We loved that! It was fun to walk forward and be given something as valuable as a dozen Titleist golf balls or something as mundane as a bottle of aerosol bug repellant donated by the local chemical company.

Each month this same club had a birthday party. Big, mature men were seated around tables. Twenty or thirty had their own individual cupcake with a candle. The master of ceremonies would read their names, tell a brief joke, and each man would light his candle. Then the other 300 of us would sing 'Happy Birthday'. This seemed so juvenile 11 months of the year. But when my birthday month of May rolled around, I never missed the party! We all love and need recognition.

They say that the definition of a preacher is 'a person who will fly across the country to preach a sermon but will not walk across the street to hear one'. We too have our enormous needs for recognition, so great that they sometimes get us into trouble.

The following is a true story. I have combined several situations into one, changing the geography of the schools and the names of the people so as to protect their anonymity.

Joe Senior is a graduate of the University of Pennsylvania and Yale Law School. Joe Junior is 17. The dream of Joe Senior is that Joe Junior will go to a fine college, a top law school and ultimately work into his law firm. There is only one problem. Joe Junior has no apparent aptitude for law. In fact, he has very little inclination toward academic pursuits of any kind. Joe Senior constantly rides him, trying to motivate him to academic excellence. He has used pressure, insult, compliment, and even bribery to achieve his goal. It's all to no avail. Let me tell you something about Joe Junior. You know what he can do? He can lift the hood of a car and take apart everything under that hood and put it back together again blindfolded. He is brilliant in mechanical matters. But never once has Joe Senior given him recognition for his abilities. We all know that the world can use more fine, honest, Christian lawyers. Frankly, we all know that the world is in even more desperate need for fine, honest, Christian automobile mechanics whose work can be trusted! This young man is gifted – gifted by God. He is starved of recognition. It breaks my heart to see what is happening to these two people.

It breaks my heart because I already know the probable end to this story. It is one of mutual resentment, bitter outbursts, and ultimate alienation.

As a pastor, I watch these sad situations develop. Sometimes I stumble into them two or three decades later.

One friend of mine has been a misfit in the ministry when he could have been an outstanding artist. His father and mother had dreams for him. He failed to recognize his true gifts.

Another friend resisted that family pressure. From his earliest years he remembered his parents praying for his future ministry. At his birth, they had set him aside for full-time Christian service as a pastor or a missionary. The only problem was this was not his calling. He was a gifted craftsman. Rebellion was his only way out. Today he is doing what he wants to do, but at the price of breaking his parents' hearts. It didn't have to be that way. If only they, his father in particular, would have recognized the unique, God-given gifts that were his. If only his dad could have celebrated the uniqueness of his son.

One Sunday I was preaching in another church as a guest. I shared these four emotional needs of intimate response, adventure, security and recognition. After the service, a bright, attractive woman in her late thirties came up to me and thanked me for the message. Wanting her to be specific, I asked her what she had found most helpful. She responded, 'You helped me decide to get a divorce.' In shock, I asked, 'How?' She answered, 'I just realized that my husband doesn't meet one of my emotional needs!'

Needless to say, that is not my point. Granted, we all have needs that are important. I am encouraging you to take the initiative to meet the emotional needs of others. In the process of doing that, I am convinced that at least some of your own needs will be met. Jesus was very clear in saying the one who wishes to be the master ends up the servant. The one who is willing to be the servant ends up being the master. The one who wants to be first will end up last. The one who is willing to be last will end up first. That's the economy of the spiritual kingdom of God. I am convinced it is also the economy of the emotional kingdom of God.

You and your loved ones have these basic emotional needs of intimate response, adventure, security, and recognition. Why don't you ask the Holy Spirit to etch these four needs on your mind and your heart so that you are constantly aware of your privilege and responsibility to meet these needs?

You may be asking, 'What good does it do to know these needs? What I need is some practical advice about how to meet them. You preachers are great at describing the situation. I need some handles.' All right, here are several. I am certain that you can come up with many more.

The first suggestion is for husbands: *Why not try dating your wife?*

You used to do it. How long has it been since you called her and asked her out? No, that business dinner doesn't count. That social obligation of a couple of nights ago when you went over to the Smiths isn't a date. Think back to when you were courting. The last thing you wanted to do was go out on a double date. You wanted to be alone together. There was adventure, security, recognition, and, dare I say, quite a bit of intimate response on those special occasions. Now you can settle into a drab, boring, marriage routine. Or you can bring it to life by concentrating on romance. Many young people today say, 'What difference does a piece of paper make? Why get married? A wedding certificate only seems to spoil romance instead of encourage it.' These young men and women know what they are talking about. They have observed adults, some being their own parents, who seem to have lost the spontaneity of love because they've not been working at bringing excitement to the relationship.

Pick up the phone. Call her from work. She may be at work herself. Ask her what she is doing Thursday night. After she recovers from cardiac arrest, she'll respond. You know what she'll be doing Thursday night. She knows what she'll be doing Thursday night. It will probably be the same old thing – the dishes. Ask her if she'd like to go out on a date. Don't make the mistake of asking her where she wants to go. Women aren't built that way. They would rather have you make the plans. If you ask her where she wants to go and keep urging her to tell you and she finally, timidly suggests a place, your response will probably be, 'Oh, we went there two weeks ago with the Smiths.' She's apt to snap, 'Then you suggest a place.' Needless to say she's not going to automatically view your place any more favorably. Soon you are back into petty wrangling. Instead, tell her where you want to take her and what time you'll pick her up. I'll guarantee you, you will have touched some of the basic emotional needs of your wife if you do it with sincerity and spontaneity.

The second suggestion is for wives: *Think about what your husband likes best and do it for him.*

I mean turn him on in every area, including the sexual. We talk too little about this from the pulpit. Every magazine and newspaper we pick up is loaded with sex. Why? Because it's a normal, healthy part of life. Certainly it can be exploited, abused and degraded. The Bible has a lot to say about sex, God is all in favor of it. He created it. Don't be afraid to think of ways in which you can stimulate your marriage partner, bringing both of you joy and gratification.

It can all start with something as simple as cooking your husband's favorite meal. When was the last time you cooked it for him? Did you tell him about it in advance? Or did you surprise him with it? The most drab time of day can be at 6:30 or 7:00 in the evening. It can also be the most exciting when two people who have worked hard all day and are exhausted are able to pause a moment and exchange a kiss and a hug as a symbol of their oneness in marriage and in Christ. You can help unwind each other, turning an average evening into a special time.

I am a lousy cook. To be honest, I am not even interested in cooking. However, I have made a mediocre stab at turning the tables around a bit, occasionally surprising Anne with something culinary. During the 1980s, she went back to school, and for the last 10 years has been a psychotherapist and now is a psychoanalyst. Monday is my day off. It is a working day for her. Occasionally, I will surprise her with something as simple as take-out pizza with a homemade tossed salad served by candlelight. Does she ever love it! Every so often, the menu changes to something a bit more complex, like a steak or a piece of salmon cooked on the outdoor barbecue accompanied by a baked potato with sour cream and chives and a tossed salad. This is followed by vanilla ice cream topped off with raspberries. Again, it's by candlelight. And I do the dishes. Never once has she complained about the cooking or that I spent half the day playing golf!

Anne and I have discovered that the best sex occurs when there is emotional and spiritual oneness. Some of that coolness, that distance, that lack of eagerness to share in physical love comes from our insensitivity to each other's emotional needs. Anne and I have found that our best love making comes when we have genuinely been making love in conversation, attitude, sharing throughout the entire evening. Sex, in its highest God-given dimension, is the ultimate expression that says that the two of us love each other all the time, even though we may have our disagreements, misunderstandings, and our differences. In this act of union we express the blending of our emotional, spiritual and physical lives.

The third suggestion is for parents: *Take your child out alone on a regular basis.*

Fathers, in particular, can benefit from this suggestion. I picked it up years ago from Dr. Charles Shedd. Early in his son Peter's life, Charlie Shedd began to have a monthly luncheon date just to be alone with his son. He continued this all through Peter's growing up days.

I was so impressed with Dr. Shedd's enthusiastic endorsement of this plan that in 1970 I started it with my oldest daughter, Suzanne. She was two-and-a-half years old at the time. At first I thought I was crazy for even thinking I could have a viable conversation with a little girl that young. Anyway, I tried.

I called her one day from the office and asked her out on a date. I had to explain that she should get dressed up, and I would pick her up at noon. Did she ever get excited! Anne got her all dressed up. She looked beautiful, waiting there in the front yard when I arrived. We went to a little English pub-style restaurant, Daddy and his little daughter. She was handed a menu by the hostess. She handled it with the same expertise as she had seen her mother handle a menu. Pretending to be able to read it, she displayed the same hesitancy and indecision, studying it carefully, until suddenly she blurted out, 'a hamburger, fries, and a Coke.' Then came the moment of truth. The menus were lowered. Daddy and Suzanne were all alone together. Much to my surprise, I found out that a two-and-a-half-year-old can carry on a fine conversation when left alone with an adult. We had a great time getting to know each other in special ways. Halfway through the lunch, Suzanne asked, 'Hey, Daddy, when are we going to eat the date?' 'You don't understand, Suzanne, this is a different kind of a date. You don't eat it. We are on it.' With that, she twisted around until she could look at the seat underneath her, trying to find the date she was on.

How exciting it has been during the past 30 years plus to have continuing times of father-daughter intimacy with Suzanne, Carla and Janet. We got to know each other, entering into a conversational style of life. It has taken discipline on my part to do this. It takes time. It takes energy. And now it takes an adjustment of not only my busy schedule, but sometimes theirs that are even busier.

I kept up that monthly schedule until finally each of the girls were launched into adult life. The bonding of all those years of monthly dates have paid rich dividends. Suzanne spent the last semester of her senior year at Princeton University struggling with Hodgkin's Disease, and then she continued the battle until her death 15 months after her graduation. I'd take no amount of money in exchange for those memories.

Those times together are a bit different now. In the case of my middle daughter, Carla, they are much less frequent, as she has long been on her own. But there was that 10 days spent together, taking her with me on a World Vision trip to Tanzania, Kenya, and Uganda the summer of 1998. Visits to World Vision projects were punctuated by two one-day outings to game parks. And there have been those occasional going-out-of-the-way-to-be-with-Carla times during the past 15 years when she was a student at Stanford, when she worked for the law firm in Palo Alto, and while she was doing her MBA at MIT in Cambridge and hopefully on into the years ahead.

With Janet, the youngest, it's been a bit different. When Anne began grad school, Janet was still a little girl. Tuesday night was our date night through the 1980s and early 1990s until she went on to college. When she graduated she moved home and got a job. Anne works late on Tuesday nights. So it was back on with those Tuesday night father-daughter dinners.

Thank God for the memories!

My father never read a book on this. He practiced this life-style intuitively. He had an arrangement with me that if I kept up my grades at school he would take me on a once-a-year, out-of-town business trip. Ours was a strict school district in the Boston area, one of the first to prohibit parental-induced absenteeism. My dad took the bull by the horns, never faking illness to accomplish his ends. He would write to the principal: 'Part of my son's education is to be with his father. His grades are up to snuff. Next week he will be missing several days of school, accompanying me on an out-of-town business trip.'

As a result I knew my dad. I still know him. At the time I am writing this book, both he and Mom are still alive. He finally retired as a minister of visitation in 1997 at age 85. Now, in his late eighties, somewhat slowed down by a couple of transitional strokes and some arteriosclerosis, he still is one of my best friends in this world. It's because he gave himself to me. He took me seriously as a person. He made sacrifices for me all through his life. Although he made his mistakes just as we all do, he did his best to keep the lines of communication open.

Dad never had any problem telling me about the facts of life. He didn't cower in the corner, as some fathers, timidly trying to approach this sensitive topic. Why? Well, we were in Cleveland when we had our most explicit conversation. I was 12 years old. It was the last day of the religious convention Dad was attending. A bowling convention had just come into the same hotel. That night the four men in the next room, which was separated from ours by a thin wall, had rented the services of a prostitute. We could hear their demeaning conversation. Dad and I had a great talk as he described the beauty of his sexual relationship with my mother. I heard then a verbal articulation of what I had already sensed in our own home. How different it sounded from the crude, ugly goings on in the next room.

One of my church members handed me this little sheet titled 'Daddy, How Much Do You Earn Per Hour?' Its message
is poignant. It reads:

> 'Daddy, how much do you earn per hour?' asked the child in a
> timid voice as his father came back home from work. With a
> harsh tone, the father replied, 'Listen, Son, those are matters
> that not even your mother knows about. Don't bother me. I
> am very tired.' 'But, Daddy,' the child insisted, 'please tell me
> how much you earn per hour.' This time the father's reaction
> was less harsh, and he said, '$8 per hour.' 'Daddy, may I please
> borrow $4,' asked the child. The father got angry and spoke
> to his son. 'So that was the reason why you wanted to know
> how much I earn. Go to sleep and don't bother me, you selfish
> child.' During the night the father was meditating about the
> incident and started to feel guilty. Maybe his son needed the
> money to buy something very important. Then, wanting to
> put his conscience to rest, he went into his son's room, and
> speaking in a low tone asked his son, 'Are you asleep, Son?'
> 'No, Daddy,' he responded, half asleep. 'Here's the money that
> you asked for,' said the father. 'Thank you, Daddy,' said the
> child. At this point, he reached under his pillow and took out
> some money. 'Now I have enough, Daddy. I have $8. Would
> you sell me one hour of your time?' asked the child.

The fourth suggestion is for children: *Try doing that job for Mom
or Dad without having to be asked.*

I will guarantee you that you'll have the happiest parent in
the world. Parents don't want to nag. They don't want to put
pressure on you. Try it once, and see what happens.

A young friend of mine who is nine years old gave his mother
a very special birthday present. The envelope said, 'Coupons Re-
deemable for Taking Out Trash, Cleaning My Room, Washing
Car, Washing Dishes, Scrubbing Kitchen Floor for Mom.' Inside
were 15 coupons, artistically drawn by this youngster. Each
one specified a particular job for which it was good. Was this
recently divorced mother, now a single parent, ever turned on!

The day after her birthday she showed me this little booklet of coupons with tears of appreciation in her eyes for her son's thoughtfulness. Then, when they were all used up, she gave me the booklet because she knew other people would benefit from this experience.

The same single mother shared with me a letter she had just gotten from her daughter who was away at college. Part of it read as follows: 'On your 50th birthday, Mom, I want to wish you all the happiness you deserve. I am so thankful that I have been your daughter, because there's no one else I can think of who could have been a better mother for me.'

Talk about meeting the emotional needs for intimate response, adventure, security, and recognition. These two young people made their mother the happiest woman in the world.

The fifth suggestion is for husbands and wives: *Be faithful to your spouse.*

Sometimes life doesn't turn out quite the way we expected it to be, and our career dreams are frustrated. That was the case of Mr. Holland, played by Richard Dreyfuss, in the box-office success 'Mr. Holland's Opus.' As you probably already know, it's the life story of a young musician whose dreams of being a great composer, performer, and orchestra leader are frustrated by life's realities of family responsibility, providing a living for his wife and deaf child. He took a job teaching music in a public school in the 1950s, finally achieving success by developing an appreciation for music in four decades of students before his job was finally phased out. There was one moment in the movie that riveted viewers' attention. It came at a time when his wife was preoccupied with raising their son as well as jealous of her husband's success in the community. Mr. Holland was directing a major music presentation when seemingly out of nowhere there emerged this gorgeous high school senior coed with a crystal-clear voice. She obviously had a deep crush on Mr. Holland. He urged her to follow her dreams in show business In a moment of great temptation, she invited him to leave his wife and join her in New York City. There, in that moment of hesitation, a person caught up in life's routine, unable to realize his true professional dreams, and, at that moment, unappreciated by his wife, Mr. Holland made his decision. He recognized responsible boundaries. The young woman departed alone, and he returned home, faithful to his wife.

More of that quality is needed in this 'I've-got-to-be-me, I-have-the-right-to-my-personal-happiness' era in which we live.

Later in this book, there is a whole chapter about sex. In it, I explore what God has to say about the smart way to use this wonderful gift.

However, let me observe how vulnerable we all are to making mistakes in this area. There are some practical ways to minimize temptation and avoid compromising situations.

One, I try to discipline myself as to what I see on television when I am alone in distant hotel rooms. One way is to simply decide never to purchase a pay-per-view X-rated adult channel movie. It's hard enough to keep one's mind clean with the normal use of the remote control, using the regular channels for the late news or a sporting event.

Two, when I am overly attracted to a person of the opposite sex, I try to immediately turn that thought into a prayer, thanking God for the beauty of that person, reminding myself that she is somebody's wife, somebody's mother, somebody's sister, or somebody's daughter. I pray, 'Dear Lord, help me to think of her and treat her the way I would want any other man to think of and treat my mother, my wife, my sister, or my daughters.' A strange thing happens. I can acknowledge the beauty and channel it in healthful directions.

Three, I make it a point never to spend time alone with someone of the opposite sex in an intimate environment, either at work or in my personal life. As a pastor, this is difficult because, throughout the years, I have done a substantial amount of one-on-one pastoral counseling. I have always had an arrangement with my secretary that she can, with one brief knock, open the door and walk into the room at any time to hand me a message.

And, in recent years, when I am alone in a counseling situation, I leave the door ajar, closed enough to protect confidentiality but open enough that someone walking by can see where I am sitting. Most luncheon and dinner engagements with a person of the opposite sex are accompanied either by my wife or another person. On those few occasions where this is impossible, I simply avoid the dinner hour. If it's a luncheon occasion, I make certain it is at an up-front table at a family-type restaurant. Frankly, I've seen too many men and women I love and value not observe some of these very simple protections. What were initially innocent associations were carried out in environments that provided a slippery slope and led to intimate conversation, physical contact, and ultimate infidelity. Some simple barriers can be set up to minimize the temptation. And God's promise in 1 Corinthians 10:13 is available to any one of us in any situation. 'No temptation has seized you except what is common to man. And God is faithful; he will not let you be tempted beyond what you can bear. But when you are tempted, he will also provide a way out so that you can stand up under it.'

The sixth suggestion is for all of us: *Cheer on your loved ones.*

Ten years ago, our daughter, Suzanne, was a senior playing volleyball at Newport Harbor High. Our family went to practically all the games. Our daughter, Janet, was at that time ten. I have one most vivid memory of that entire season in which Newport Harbor ended up ranked second in the nation and runner-up at the state championship. I can hear it as if it was today, that clear encouraging voice of Janet, so sincerely calling out among all the rest of the cheering crowd, 'You can do it, Harbor! You can do it, Harbor!' She was cheering on her sister, whom she loved so much, and all of her sister's friends.

People like that are those whom Tom Tewell, pastor of the Fifth Avenue Presbyterian Church in New York City, calls 'Balcony People'. Take some of your discretionary time to give encouragement to others. You and I can be balcony people for our family members, both nuclear and extended, cheering, 'You can do it! You can do it!'

Try experimenting. Come up with your own suggestions. There are so many ways that you and I, with the help of Jesus Christ, can increasingly provide for the emotional needs of those we love!

It's difficult to meet the emotional needs of others if your own emotional needs are not being met. And there are times when we all confront those vacuum moments of emotional emptiness.

It is at times like these that I talk to God in conversational prayer. I tell him honestly how I am feeling. I tell him how empty I am, how emotionally unfulfilled.

When that doesn't work, I begin to journal. I write my private thoughts as a prayer, being brutally honest with God, expressing to him my doubts, my questions, my temptations, reminding him and myself of times when I felt better and where the circumstances were better. Then, to supplement all this, especially when my prayers feel like they are bouncing back at me, I open the Bible to familiar passages. One in particular gives me great comfort. I picture men and women of faith through all the ages surrounding me in an arena, cheering me on in my own life and my efforts to meet the emotional needs of those entrusted to me. I read aloud these following words of Hebrews 12:1-3:

> Therefore, since we are surrounded by such a great cloud of witnesses, let us throw off everything that hinders and the sin that so easily entangles, and let us run with perseverance the race marked out for us. Let us fix our eyes on Jesus, the author and perfecter of our faith, who for the joy set before him endured the cross, scorning its shame, and sat down at the right hand of the throne of God. Consider him who endured such opposition from sinful men, so that you will not grow weary and lose heart.

# CHAPTER 6
## GETTING ALONG WITH YOUR CHILDREN —
## AND LOVING THEM IN THE PROCESS

*Fathers, do not embitter your children, or they will become discouraged*

Colossians 3:21

Columnist Janet Chusmir writes:

It has gotten so that I hesitate to ask about the children.

I hesitate with friends because it will open wounds. And with strangers, because so often it ends up that I'm treading on their painful and embarrassing ground.

Once, a woman I was interviewing brought the subject around to her daughter. 'I like my daughter. I respect her. I enjoy being with her,' she said with such warmth and joy and enthusiasm that I – taken by surprise – wrote her words down in my notebook. Liking, respecting, enjoying a child.... That was news.

Children are actually divorcing their parents at an enormously high rate. For some strange reason, many children don't want to have anything to do with them. This, of course, goes for teenagers. It also applies to many married individuals in their twenties, thirties, and forties who would rather not be around their parents.

I am noticing a phenomenon that has developed in recent years that I did not observe thirty years ago when I began writing and speaking about the family. I find myself talking to more and more men and women, especially women in their late thirties through midfifties – who were the ideal compliant children, teenagers, and young adults – who are now deeply immersed in therapy and engaged in highly problematic relationships with their aging parents. I listen to the stories from both generations. Sometimes these middle-aged adult children express their frustration with their parents in ways that show at least an attempt to understand them. More often I hear statements of unbridled anger and observe actions that appear much like adolescent rebellion delayed by twenty or thirty years. And I hear words of sad lament from parents, now in their sixties, seventies, and even eighties, which range all the way from the wistful, 'Granted, we made our mistakes, but we really tried to do our best,' to angry protestations, 'We raised her to be such a happy child, gave her every opportunity. How can she now be so ungrateful in attacking me this way?'

The Bible says, 'Fathers, do not exasperate your children; instead, bring them up in the training and instruction of the Lord' (Eph. 6:4).

Is this not the biggest problem in getting along with your children and still loving them in the process? We love our children, whatever their age and circumstances of life may be. We want the best for them. Providing that best is one of the toughest problems in the world. So often our finest plans backfire. What hurts more than when children, whatever age, fling resentment, anger and rebellion toward their parents?

I believe that you and I can get along with our children and still love them in the process. Paul wrote to the Colossian Christians: 'Fathers, do not embitter your children, or they will become discouraged' (Col. 3:21). The New English Bible translates those words as follows: 'Fathers, do not exasperate your children, for fear they grow up disheartened.' The New Revised Standard Version translation: 'Fathers, do not provoke your children, or they may lose heart.'

There are ways that we make our children hostile. There are ways that we make them discouraged. It doesn't matter how old they are, they still are our children, and we can creatively learn new ways to better relate to them. I heard a man in his fifties introduce another man in his sixties to a group of us the other day as 'a man with whom I meet regularly to discuss how we can be better parents to our adult children'. These men are on to something exciting.

I'd like to share with you a checklist of six basic questions that can help revolutionize your relationship with your children. I write not as an expert but as a learner. I don't have all the answers. I hope you can take what I say in the spirit of a fellow experimenter who is willing to express his own weaknesses, fears, failures, and aspirations – one who is willing to grow along with you.

Question one: *Do I really take my child seriously as a person?*
How much attention are you paying to your youngster? Do you view your children as a group? Or are you involved with them as individuals. Do you really know your children as individual persons?

It is exciting to understand the biblical teaching about God's love for you and me. There is a covenant relationship in which God treats us as a group. We are his family. But God is interested in you as a person. He loves you so much that he went to the cross for you, not just for humankind. He takes a personal interest in you. He gives you his full attention. He ministers to your individual needs. He even knows the number of hairs on your head! He sets the pattern for the parent-child relationship.

Are you spending time alone with each of your children? Earlier in the book, I talked about 'dating' your children. And I have referred primarily to the father-child relationship. I think it is especially important for those of us who are fathers, who are not at home that much, to get to know our children as individuals.

However, this is important not only for the father but for the mother too. This involves not only working mothers, who are out of the home for long periods of time, it also involves stay-at-home moms. It is so easy for you mothers who spend all day with your children to get caught up in a group psychology. You observe your child. You know each one's personality traits. How often do you spend some time alone with that child, building the bridge of personal understanding, personal relationship, so that she feels free to talk with you as an individual apart from brother or sister? How important it is to emphasize an equality of love! How we need the guidance of God's Holy Spirit to be sensitive to balance within the home, providing love and tenderness that meets the needs of each of our children – realizing that these needs are shifting and this balance can easily be thrown out of kilter.

One thing I've had to discover is the importance of being available on my child's time schedule, not just my own. Busy fathers know that we must schedule time for our family. If we don't, we'll not be with our children very often. I had to discover, though, that my children were not always ready for me when I was ready for them. Sometimes they were ready for me when I was not ready for them.

Dr. Charlie Shedd, a popular writer about family relationships, who had a great impact on me during my early child-raising days, relates an incident between him and his then four-year-old daughter, Karen. He had promised a committee chairman at his church that he would meet him early before a committee meeting. As he rushed toward the front door, Karen called out, 'Daddy, will you read to me?' Shedd tells how the usual excuses formed on his lips, but he blurted out, 'Sure, honey, I'll read to you.' So he stopped and read. It couldn't have been more than three minutes. Then he closed the book and said, 'Gee, that's an exciting story. I can hardly wait to see how it comes out. Do you think you can wait?' 'Oh,' said Karen, 'I already know how it comes out. Mommy reads that one all the time.' Shedd makes his point. How blind can a daddy be? Karen didn't want to know what the book said. She wanted something else. She longed to know that she mattered more to her daddy than some 'dumb old committee meeting at the church'.

When was the last time you crawled into your child's skin? When was the last time you identified with the kind of thought going on with that teenager who is in the turmoil of becoming an adult? When was the last time you took as seriously his romantic problems as you take your own? When was the last time you viewed her symbols of status – whether makeup, hairstyle, clothing or music tastes – as seriously as you take yours, as smart, attractive, and entertaining as they are? When was the last time you got down on your knees and looked around at the world to see how big it all seems and how awesome it is from that toddler's perspective? When was the last time you tried to identify with the pressures facing that single adult child in her late twenties who is trying to balance career with aspirations of marriage, home and children?

We need to see our children as people who have a right to know what we are thinking and why we are so firm on some matters.

Don Shula, at the height of his successful coaching career with the Miami Dolphins, said this about his relationship with individual players:

> The word I stress is communication. I try to always keep the doors of communication open. Then when you do make a decision, players will accept it more readily than they would if you are dogmatic. They tend to reject dogma. I did as a player.

Our children want to know why. They want to see the real us. They don't want dogma. They want a real personal sharing.

Child expert Dr. Bruno Bettelheim was once asked why so many parents don't like their children, why they find them such a problem. His response was that the problem is not one of parents and children not liking each other. Instead, it is that 'they don't know each other'.

To fail to see my child as a person who needs individual attention is to provoke my child to wrath, to rebellion. Some day that child will cry out, 'I'm ME. Take ME seriously. Love ME. Know ME. Care for ME.' He may never do it out loud. But he'll grab your attention somehow by actions that will demand that you take him seriously. He will act out in some way that requires you to show him the attention he needs. This may be the acting out of a child, a teenager, a young adult, or perhaps someone even in middle age, who will communicate their message in unmistakable form.

Question two: *Do I really care enough to make any sacrifice for my children?*

I think we need to ask ourselves just how far we are willing to go for the sake of our family. I wonder how often our concerns for our children are actually selfish. Yes, we love them. At the same time, we don't want to be burdened by their misconduct. We are readily willing to turn their care over to others so as to be free to do the things we like to do.

A generation ago we talked about mothers who felt confined by staying at home, who yearned to break out of the domesticated confinement of those four walls. Now the traditional housewife and mother is a much smaller percentage of society. We are forced to reconsider how we express our gender-related roles. In many ways they have become quite blurred. Some lament the fact that women are working outside of the home and idealize a simpler era when mother's work was in the home and father's work was outside of the home. But now, at least, we are able to face up to the fact that both father and mother bear responsibility for the welfare of the family. For most of us, the day is over in which we can simply delegate to the woman the responsibility of raising the children and delegate to the man the responsibility of providing financially for the family.

Both husband and wife are privileged to face the reality that our highest contribution to society is not our work outside of the home. Our highest calling in the world is to produce an environment in which our children are given the viable option of loving God, themselves, and others. Our vocations that produce our financial income are important – but not as important as our vocational calling to be followers of Jesus and servants of our family members. Is there any greater opportunity in life than to invest in our families?

Are you frustrated by the demands of family living? Do you yearn for that single era in your life when you were free from the constant demands of being a father or a mother? I am much more frequently meeting men and women who are consciously, or perhaps subconsciously, endeavoring to avoid responsible leadership in the home. They resent the interruption on their time and careers caused by children. At the same time, I am talking with more and more middle-aged adults who, because they have postponed the starting of a family, feel the biological clock ticking and regret the fact that they have postponed so long child raising.

Is your work getting in the way of your family? Is your recreation taking you away from your children to the point that you don't really know them?

Some time ago, the *Today* show carried a fascinating interview with Dr. James Windle, professor of management supervision at Purdue University. He was talking about his theory of the 'I-don't-give-a-damn syndrome'. He said that there is a contagious attitude rapidly spreading in which people are paying less and less attention to doing responsible work. This is why a brand-new car breaks down so quickly. This is why when we put on a sport coat or dress we find that the buttons are mismatched and the lining is sloppily sewn. Windle is convinced that no amount of management effort toward job enrichment, rotation, shorter workweek, flexible work schedules, and many of the other temporary solutions will actually solve the problem. A person has to have a deep sense of commitment to one's work. It must be seen as a top priority, not just a boring routine to somehow provide bread for the table.

How far are you and I willing to go for the sake of our children? Are we willing to make sacrifices? Are we willing to adjust the economic life of our family, our lifestyles, to see that our children are in the right environment? Are we willing to change our social relationships if we find that our present friendships or associations are having a derogatory effect? Or is our economic and social lifestyle more important than our children are?

My father relates with great joy the fact that his father left his teaching job to move to another college at lower pay because he sensed his oldest son needed a new environment. Whether the move solved the problem, I don't know. What I do know is that my father, a quarter of a century later, takes pride in his father's willingness to personally sacrifice for his family.

We need to be honest as to whether we are willing to make the sacrifice of discipline, prayer and concern for our children. Or are we, without realizing it, caught up in the I-don't-give-a-damn syndrome? I know that in one way we really care. But is that more than rhetoric? Are we neglecting rigorous priorities, forgetting that the greatest contribution you and I can make to this world is not our vocational or social success but children who have the opportunity to know what it is to love Christ, who are as well adjusted as possible and who are able to serve, with enthusiasm, their God and fellow human beings? Not to really care enough to make whatever sacrifice we are called on to make is to provoke our child to wrath, to agitate that young person to the point of discouragement. Our children know instinctively where our priorities are and what distance we are willing to go in sacrifice.

Question three: *Are you giving your child too much attention?*
You take children seriously not just by giving them undivided, individual attention. You also need to be sensitive to when to stay away and how to stay away.

I have to ask myself the question, 'Do I pay too much attention at times to my children?' I have to answer the question, 'Yes.' I have the tendency to compulsively demand their attention not on their schedule but on my schedule in ways that tend to consume them with an overwhelming smothering affection.

It's important to let the real person develop. Sometimes we act as if we want to create robots. We pick the outstanding young person in the school, neighborhood, church, and we point out that individual as a paragon of virtue to our own youngster. 'Why can't you be like Johnny Jones? He is such a good, hard worker. He takes the trash out for his mother. He is so courteous. He always looks neat.'

I need to remember something quite exciting. It is this. God is not in the business of creating robots. Think that through. He has created only one you. God is in the business of helping you realize your creative potential to the very fullest. How does it feel when someone tries to squeeze you into their mold? It's not very comfortable, is it? You don't feel valued when your husband asks, 'Why don't you dress like …?' and names that one person who you don't really care for that much. How do you feel when your wife compares what you provide materially – the car, home, furniture, and status – to what that other fellow gives his wife? Our kids respond the same way. They are individual creations of God with all kinds of creative potential.

One great commandment could be added to the other ten: 'Thou shalt not frustrate the holy in thy child!' Isn't that really what the Apostle Paul is saying when he says, 'Fathers, do not embitter your children, or they will become discouraged' (Col. 3:21).

This is probably one of the toughest jobs we have as parents – to let the real person develop. We tend to have a perverted need to somehow manage the lives of our children, no matter how old they are.

Charlie Shedd, in his book titled *Promises to Peter*, makes some suggestions that can revolutionize your whole concept of responsible parenthood. In one chapter titled *I've Got to Be Me* he states that one of the first jobs of a parent is to be able to say and mean this:

Listen, my children! Your first loyalty is not to me. In you there is a native self. The secret is to discover who God wants you to be and be true to that. This moment I set you free to say, 'Get off my back. I've got to be me!'

Even if you don't take this approach, ultimately, your children are going to demand this of you. How much better is it if they don't have to rebel to realize exactly who they are. How much better to be guided and loved into becoming their own people?

Question four: *Do I really love my child enough to provide firm discipline?* This business about allowing children to become their own people doesn't mean giving them too much freedom. It means being responsive to the development and growth of our youngsters. Every child needs rules.

Frankly, I believe that the goal of parenthood should be to respect our children to the point where we help them grow beyond us so that at age 18 they are capable of making the major decisions of life for themselves. Hopefully, with our counsel, they'll mature enough to be adult. At the same time, a 13-year-old is not an 18-year-old. This needs to be kept in balance. Too many teenagers are suffering from an overdose of self-government.

One young woman writes:

My problem is probably one you don't hear much. My daddy is a doctor and he is so busy. My mother is a champion golfer and she is at the club every afternoon when I come home from school. On weekends they party and sometimes I worry about it, that they drink too much, especially lately. But what really bothers me is how they let me do almost anything I want to. They never tell me when to come in, and I can go anywhere. You might think how lucky she is. But I tell you that is not how I feel about it. What bothers me is I wonder if I am all that ready to decide everything by myself.

As a young person increasingly shows maturity, we must give her freedom to make her own decisions – right or wrong – but at the same time we need to realize that the truest freedom functions within the loving confines of some specific guidelines.

I am aware that as a culture we have moved quite a way away from the era in which the child was usually disciplined with a spanking. We are desperately fearful of being accused of child abuse. If we are going to err on any side, I certainly would suggest that we should avoid any discipline that is done in a way that is overbearing, insensitive, and carried out in anger. However, Proverbs 13:24 must not be scissored out of the Bible. It declares: 'He who spares the rod hates his son, but he who loves him is careful to discipline him.' Proverbs 23:13-14 reads: 'Do not withhold discipline from a child; if you punish him with the rod, he will not die. Punish him with the rod and save his soul from death.'

Some of us are too harsh, totally dominating our children and leaving them in a constant state of fear. On the other hand, some of us are too permissive. Firm discipline develops respect for a parent, which is important because it determines all the future relationships of that child's life. You may choose not to use spankings. But you and I must have some kind of discipline reserved for a direct expression of self-will on the part of the child when that little one declares, 'I will not,' in rebellion against parental authority. Instead of closing channels of communication, firm, loving punishment – which comes across primarily as consequences – actually opens freedom of expression. Immediately following firm discipline in love, the average child is most open to expressions of love, understanding, and the warm embrace of the parent.

Sometimes we are scared of our children. We are afraid that our discipline will turn them against us. The opposite is true. Our failure to discipline is the clear sign that we don't care enough.

God cares for you and me. Sometimes he disciplines us. Often there is pain in his reproof. In the process, he bends us from our way to his way, alerting us to our need of his love, his grace, his authority. He cares that much for us. Do we care that much for our children?

Question five: *Do I see my child as every bit as important as myself?* This may be the most important question of all.

I find it very difficult at times to view my children with the objectivity I need to have to see them as autonomous human beings. In one way, they are an extension of who I am. As a result, they are very, very important. But would I see them as important if I looked at them as if they were your son or your daughter?

In some ways, you and I are able to see the children of others as just as important as ourselves more easily than to see our own children that way. What do I mean by this? What I mean is that our basic human narcissism tends to see our children as extensions of ourselves in a way that elevates them to a disproportionally high importance that comes from that self-identity we have with them. As a result, there are moments in which we look down on them because they come from us. At other times, we put them on a pedestal because they become a unique and special expression of who we are. If I read the Bible correctly, I see every human being as created in the image of God and equal in God's sight. If that is the case, my child and your child, you and I, and every human being in this world is important. Each is no more important than we are nor any less important.

It is easy to reflect on this and conclude that it's right. The real question is whether we have conveyed this sense of importance to our children.

I have to be honest. I have a sneaking suspicion that if my two daughters were looking over my shoulder right now, reading these words, they would probably roll their eyes at each other, in essence saying, 'Can you believe Dad is saying this?' I don't know this for certain. But I do know that they think that I think I am very important. And I do know that Anne and I have been somewhat awesome figures in their lives. Somehow you and I have to get across to our children, at whatever age they are, that they are no less and no more important than anyone else and, in particular, they are every bit as important as you and me.

Question six: *Do I really love my child enough to ultimately let go?*
You and I, whether we realize it or not, can be masters of invasive behavior.

Some of us parents have a CIA mentality with our children.
We do not respect the sanctity of their privacy. We are snoops.
We are eavesdroppers. We are letter readers. You know what
that does to us as adults? You and I don't want people check-
ing out our every activity, do we? Nor does your youngster.
I do want people to love me, to be available to me. Yet I am
a private individual. I want to have the right to share my in-
nermost thoughts about myself. I tend to share them not with
people who demand them of me but with the people who accept me. I want to share with people with whom I feel secure,
by whom I am loved. Children want parents who are willing
to be available, yet who are not snoopers. A parent willing to
be available and yet not snoop will learn more with less grief.
Kids know how to hide. They can do a beautiful job of cover-up
if they think their every step is being traced. Yet a youngster
who knows his parents care is free to express himself in fresh
communications. To fail to respect the private areas as a parent
is to provoke your child's wrath.

I am not just talking about teenagers. I am having to learn
this lesson with my adult children. I find myself at times asking
questions that are invasive of my daughter who is in her mid-
twenties. Fortunately, she doesn't let me get by with it. She has
the strength of character to speak up and say, 'Dad, that's my
personal business.' And I have to learn how not to pout when
she is very direct in declaring some question I've asked about
her or one of her friends as being inappropriate. After all, she is
used to this dad and the games we play in family relationships
where we control and manipulate in such subtle ways. I can
say that I really love my child enough to ultimately let her go.
The fact that I've said it doesn't mean that I've conveyed that
as a feeling to her.

In a way, we are given our children, are we not? We cup
them gently in our hands. The ultimate goal is to open our

hands fully so that they can walk away, no strings attached, and someday turn around and walk back to us, rediscovering us as adult friends.

I don't like to have friendships where there are strings attached, do you? I like to be able to look eyeball to eyeball, in a quality of relationship, at another adult person. We accept each other in our humanity, as equals created in the image of God, responsible directly to Him for who we are and not responsible to that other adult who is lording it over me.

That's why I am so impressed when Jesus told that story about the father who had the rebel son, who let the son go. He doesn't force the son to come home; nor does he manipulate the self-righteous older brother into compliance. He loves both sons. He yearns to be in fellowship with both of them and to have them love each other. However, he doesn't force the issue.

He is not like the father in the movie *Shine*, who – frustrated by his own desires of being a concert violinist – tries to realize his dreams through his son who was an extremely gifted pianist. It is the true story of pianist David Helfgott. How I saw in that father on the screen my own tendency to flesh out my own dreams through my children. I can manipulate with strings of money, affection, affirmation, and emotional support when they do what I want, and with the questioning look and the guilt-inducing question when they don't do what I want. Thank God for his model of unconditional love that welcomes me home into relationship with him, that challenges me to a high standard of life because I know I am accepted in the Beloved.

My dream for myself and for you is that we may be able to really, authentically, get along with our children, whatever age they may be, and love them in the process.

CHAPTER 7
WHAT A GODLY PARENT LOOKS LIKE

*I prayed for this child, and the Lord has granted me what I asked of him. So now I give him to the Lord. For his whole life he will be given over to the Lord*

1 Samuel 1:27-28

Most of us come to parenting without much preparation. That's an understatement, isn't it?

Sometimes we come to parenting with very inadequate models.

A few years back, a member of our church sent me a copy of his family history. I had known this man for most of two decades. I'd watched him grow in his Christian faith as a husband, as a father, as a hard-working breadwinner for his family. At the same time, I had watched him struggle, at times intensely, with emotional illness. In the last few years, he had done much better at coping. It helped that he had some family research and realized the acute dysfunction from which he had been fortunate to emerge. He and his wife wanted to share with me the specifics of his family history, which revealed several generations who had suffered from alcoholism, depression, and severe mental illness that led, in several cases, to suicide. His final observation was that he wanted to do whatever he could to break this cycle. I admired him for it.

Ours is a society searching for parenting models.

The very institution of fatherhood is in crisis. Many American men are disconnecting from family life, and society is paying the price. Many fathers, now divorced, are not only failing to keep up their financial responsibilities but are also abdicating their opportunity to stay in touch with their children. Seventy percent of all imprisoned U. S. minors have spent at least part of their lives without their fathers. Throughout history men have been torn from their families by war, disease, and death. But as we in America move into this new millennium, we have a phenomenon in which men are choosing to disconnect from family life on a massive scale. In some cases, men are drifting away from family life and leaving their wives or girlfriends to raise fatherless children. And there is the increasing reality of women electing to give birth to children and raise them with-out husbands. A significant percentage of Americans are being raised fatherless.

A recent article in the Los Angeles Times states:

> All across America tonight, one-third of the nation's children will go to bed without their biological fathers in the next room. And most of them won't see their fathers the next day, either. According to studies by Frank F. Furstenberg, Jr., a University of Pennsylvania sociologist, about 40% of the children who live in fatherless households haven't seen their fathers in at least a year; for many others, contact is sporadic. In any month, only one in five of these children sleep even one night in their father's home. 'It's a minority of [absent] fathers that have at least once-a-week contact,' says Furstenberg.

Harvard University psychologist Samuel Osherson has taken his own troubled relationship with his father and used it as the springboard for his search for the meaning of fatherhood. His book is titled *Finding Our Fathers: The Unfinished Business of Manhood*. He based it on his own autobiographical explorations and his clinical experience as well as a 25-year study of 370 Harvard graduates. He concludes that if you don't come to terms with past relationships, especially with your parents, you may be condemned to reproduce them. We become, in essence, the parents we swore we would never be.

He goes on then to describe a 'remote sadness' in his relationship with his own father and broadens that to conclude that very few men report a close and secure relationship with their fathers. Most men feel that their fathers lack the emotional strength to be open with their sons.

Bill Cosby wrote a best-selling book titled *Fatherhood*, in which he cast one jaundiced eye at the trials and tribulations of fatherhood, while winking impishly with the other. Cosby expressed great ambivalence about fatherhood, acknowledging an unresolved relationship with his own father. His references to him are few and unpleasant, referring to the days when 'my own father used me for batting practice'. He went on to refer to his father, never by name, as a strict and stingy tyrant, a throwback to the absolute monarchist.

You can see then how confused Cosby must have been as he came to the task of being a father himself. He writes about the essence of the good father being the total acceptance of the child for better or for worse, urging parents to keep trying and keep having patience. On the other hand, he describes a contradictory undercurrent in which he portrays children as selfish, expensive, and contrary liars, 'young adversaries'. He expressed Cosby's First Law of Intergenerational Perversity in which 'No matter what you tell a child to do, he will always do the opposite'. What I admire is the fact that Cosby has even been willing to address this complex topic given his own family background and frustration in the task.

The good news is that much is being written about fatherhood. So whereas some are dismissing fatherhood as irrelevant, others are emphasizing not only the importance of fatherhood but the enhanced nurturing roles which fathers can play. The sociologist Michael S. Kimmel has made the hopeful observation that we can '... see fathers as safe and nurturing, exactly the emotionally expressive men that feminists suggested they should become. No longer the "forgotten parent" of earlier psychological studies, father now shares center stage with mother in a flood of books about the joys of co-parenting and joint custody, or the political correctness of becoming a house-husband. In fact, mother had better be careful or she'll be pushed to the wings.'

In the first 60 years of this century in the United States we tended to eulogize mothers, putting them on a pedestal. However, with the emergence of the feminist movement and the increased opportunity, and even necessity, for women to work outside of the home, we discover an increased ambivalence about what it is to be a mother. Many articles are being written, some championing a return of mothers to the home. At the same time, researchers are advancing the concept that, even if economically possible, such a return of women to traditional mothering roles would not be healthy. The thinking is that mothers need an opportunity to express themselves, experiencing a sense of achievement in the marketplace, having an economic identity of their own.

The task of the pastor is not to be the ultimate sociologist and/or psychologist. The role of the pastor is to sensitively listen to questions people are raising, feeling the joy and pain of their lives, to be aware of one's own struggles as a spouse, a parent, and a child, and, when speaking on family matters, to articulate bottom-line, biblical principles that can be guideposts for us in our odysseys as parents.

It's important to note that there is not one father or mother in the Bible who shows us in perfect form how to be a parent. In a way that's a relief, isn't it? It takes a lot of pressure off you and me to realize that none of the biblical saints had it all together as parents. Some of them made terrible mistakes. We can learn from what some did well and what some did poorly.

I'd like to take Hannah, the mother of Samuel, as someone who presents a model for contemporary motherhood. You can read about her in 1 Samuel 1-2. Hannah emerged out of anonymity. You don't have to be in the social registry to accomplish true greatness. Her breeding was average. Her husband came from a line of unknowns. They lived in the hill country north of Jerusalem, 1,100 years before Christ.

The model we will take for a father is that sketched by Jesus in his parable that some call the 'Prodigal Son', but I would rather refer to it as the 'Waiting Father'. The story is a mirror of you and me, helping us realize how God functions as the ultimate single parent, relating to both a wayward prodigal son and a self-righteous, prideful son. This parable in its pristine beauty paints a picture of a model parent, that ideal representation of what it is to interact with one's children, giving you and me helpful insights for our significant task.

Taking Hannah and the Prodigal Son's father as role models, because they are biblical characters that come closest to perfect role models, I'd like to share with you 13 characteristics from the Bible that capture the essence of parenting. So let's begin our rapid listing that will help us see what a godly parent is, trusting this will not frustrate us with our own shortcomings but challenge us to creative possibilities of such a biblical approach to parenting. Let's view this simply as a checklist, not designed to make us feel bad, but to encourage us in areas in which we are already strong and to point out areas in which we can give creative attention, accepting the fact that effective parenting is a life-long endeavor.

One, a godly parent *gets help for his/her problems.*

Hannah certainly had her sorrows. She was one of two wives. Her husband, Elkanah, apparently took reasonably good care of her but, obviously, he had divided loyalties. Polygamy, which was tolerated under the Mosaic law, never was the original, divine intention. It inevitably provided divided loyalties, much as does the serial polygamy of today, which we call divorce. That's why Jesus articulated a higher standard (Matt. 19:3-8), knowing the misery caused by the multiplicity of spouses.

I have a friend who, the last time I saw him, had four wives. He lives in Cairo. Each time we have gotten together he laments his sad circumstances, crying, 'It's impossible to keep all four wives happy at one time.' Inevitably, each of the four vies for the position of number-one wife. He buys a gift for one; the others complain.

If polygamy is not a happy experience for a man, imagine the misery it causes for a woman. I've never seen four sadder persons than those wives of my Egyptian friend. He is king; they are slaves. They do his bidding as they vie for his attention. Hannah knew the feeling. She had to share Elkanah's affection with another woman by the name of Peninnah. Peninnah seemed to get all the breaks. Why? She had sons and daughters. Hannah was barren. There was nothing more miserable for a Hebrew woman than to be without a child. Peninnah reaped certain economic benefits as a result of her affluent childbearing. Added to Hannah's sorrow was the fact that Peninnah rubbed it in. She would mock Hannah, irritating her, implying that the closed womb resulted from divine disgrace, that the Lord had closed her womb. The pressure didn't let up. It went on year after year. Each year they would go to Shiloh to participate in the religious sacrifices. That's when it really got bad, and that's when Peninnah provoked her the most. Finally, Hannah broke down and wept. In her grief, she could not eat. The man, although a good husband, suffered from typical male chauvinism. His response to her problem was to say, 'Hannah, why are you weeping? Why don't you eat? Why are you downhearted? Don't I mean more to you than ten sons?' (1 Sam. 1:8).

Hannah sought help. She rose and went near the temple. 'In bitterness of soul Hannah wept much and prayed to the Lord' (1 Sam. 1:10). She sought God's help. She prayed for a child. Not only that. She sought help and counsel from Eli, the priest. Eli, not a perfect father himself, was a man who loved God and gave pastoral comfort, counsel, and support to this would-be parent. Although hers was not the easiest of marriages, she made the best of a tough situation. She went home and was a good wife. She acknowledged her adversity, changing what she could change while claiming God's help to handle those troubles that were unrelenting. And God ultimately blessed her with a child whom we have come to know as Samuel.

Seek God's help in your parenting. When you need it, don't hesitate to get counsel from godly friends, from pastors, from well-trained therapists.

Two, a godly parent *remains loving and lovable in spite of difficulties.* Being loving and lovable isn't always easy to achieve.

I remember listening to a cassette lecture entitled 'Christian Wives' by Gladys Hunt. She was talking about what it is to be a truly liberated woman. What particularly impressed me was the way she described how some women who have been pushed around by life tend to work out their anger on innocent persons. She told about a woman who had a heartbreaking, childhood incident. She had wanted to be cuddled in her mother's lap. Her mother rejected the girlish request. Something within that young girl died. With tears, the woman described to Mrs. Hunt how she was doing the same thing to her children that her mother did to her. She had denied all four of her children affectionate access to her lap, keeping them at arm's length.

Here is where Hannah provides a beautiful model. She refused to become hard. She remained lovable in spite of her difficulties. We see it in her relationship with her husband Elkanah. The Bible says, 'He loved Hannah ....' Knowing this, she didn't let his male chauvinism get the better of her. She remained lovable in spite of it.

How often I see wives who have been injured. They have reasonable complaints. Their husbands are insensitive and sometimes unfaithful. Their children have been ungrateful. So they build walls around their hearts. They harden themselves. They will never be hurt again. Something dies in them. Even if the husband wakes up to his mistakes and wants a second chance, there is no second chance. She has given up. She has allowed the difficulties to get the better of her, and it impacts her children.

I've seen this with men also. The child rebels. The father is turned off. What he can't control, he refuses to love. He builds a wall around his heart so that he will not be hurt again.

The father Jesus described was a father who continued to love that son who had taken an early inheritance, wasting it on wine, women, and song. He was a father who scanned the horizon, yearning for his son's return. He, like Hannah, remained vulnerable. When the son returned, he welcomed him with open arms. We'll never know how many more times he was hurt by both the rebel son and the self-righteous, critical older brother who chided that man for his wanton lovability.

Three, godly parents *live comfortably with their gender*.

Don't be ashamed to be a man. Don't be ashamed to be a woman. Be proud, in a healthy, humble way. God created you the gender that you are.

I will be the first to grant that traditional cultures have, through the centuries, exploited women. Even sincere, Christian teaching has too often forced non-biblical role models upon women, insisting that all women be the same, declaring her place is in the home, nowhere else. Fortunately, some of these non-biblical attitudes are breaking down.

I am convinced that secular society, with all of its heralded women's liberation, has only intensified its exploitation. On one hand, men increasingly use women as sexual objects, not persons. Men are trading in wives of 15 to 30 years for brand-new nubile models, crassly forgetting that there is a difference between a mannequin and a person. On the other hand, there is that non-Christian feminism that elevates a unisex ideal, with women dressing just like men and acting like men, demanding a sameness that denies that uniqueness given by God when he created male and female. Male and female are equal before God, but they are not the same. There is no way in the world that I can have a baby. I will never experience either the pain or the ecstasy. My wife Anne and I are equal before God, but we are not identical.

Hannah wasn't ashamed of being a woman. She wanted to be a woman who experienced all that was part of being female. She didn't want just to be an extension of her husband. She wanted to be a whole person.

The older I get the more I realize some of the limitations I have by being a male, and the limitations that I'm unaware of are quickly pointed out by a contemporary society that is increasingly critical of male idiosyncrasies.

Read the Bible carefully, and you will discover model women and men who were not afraid to express their femaleness and maleness in healthy ways and also stay in touch with some of those feelings that are more quickly identified with the opposite gender.

That father Jesus told about in the parable, although a manly man, was free to show his emotions. Hannah, although living in a patriarchal environment, refused to simply be an extension of her husband. She saw herself as a person. She had individuality. She understood her intrinsic worth. She had the boldness to approach God as a person. She had self-worth in spite of her difficulties. And God accepted her on those terms. She didn't have to come through her husband. She was a very special person to God – and so are you, and so am I.

Four, a godly parent *teaches truth from infancy on up.*
Jesus did not tell this story about the father in a vacuum. He was telling it to Jews. Jews knew the Old Testament Scriptures. Basic to their great heritage was the parental responsibility to expose their children to the teachings of the Scriptures, both in precept and in action. Just before entering the Promised Land, Moses reminded the people of Israel:

> Hear, O Israel: The Lord our God, the Lord is one. Love the Lord your God with all your heart and with all your soul and with all your strength. These commandments that I give you today are to be upon your hearts. Impress them on your children. Talk about them when you sit at home and when you walk along the road, when you lie down and when you get up. Tie them as symbols on your hands and bind them on your foreheads. Write them on the doorframes of your houses and on your gates (Deut. 6:4-9).

Discipline is essential to this teaching. Moses incorporated these words into his address: 'Know then in your heart that as a man disciplines his son, so the Lord your God disciplines you' (Deut. 8:5). He is calling mothers and fathers to live under the authority of God's teaching, modeling for our children what it is to live disciplined lives. As we live under God's authority, what we teach our children about the ways of God takes on more existential relevance to them. If I teach them one mode of conduct and live under a different mode myself, they will see the hypocrisy of it all.

Moses adds an additional dimension to this. He knows that the people will be more receptive to God's ways in difficult times as they are coming out of the wilderness experience. He warns them that there will be some days of prosperity ahead.

Be careful that you do not forget the Lord your God, failing to observe his commands, his laws and his decrees that I am giving you this day. Otherwise, when you eat and are satisfied, when you build fine houses and settle down, and when your herds and flocks grow large and your silver and gold increase and all you have is multiplied, then your heart will become proud and you will forget the Lord your God, who brought you out of Egypt, out of the land of slavery (Deut. 8:11-14).

Five, a godly parent *gives the child back to the Lord.*
Children are very much a gift from God. Those of you who have had difficulty getting pregnant know how true this is. You know Hannah's anguish. There is nothing like that pain. How badly she wanted a child. And now it is only complicated by abortion on demand. How quickly so many dispense with life, making it very difficult for those who yearn to adopt.

Hannah finally had a baby. What an exciting time for her. We observe a fascinating statement she makes when finally little Samuel is weaned. She took him up to Shiloh. She and Elkanah brought the child to Eli. She said to the priest:

'As surely as you live, my lord, I am the woman who stood here beside you praying to the Lord. I prayed for this child, and the Lord has granted me what I asked of him. So now I give him to the Lord. For his whole life he will be given over to the Lord' (1 Sam. 1:26-28).

What enormous lessons Hannah and Elkanah teach mothers and fathers of every age. You and I have the responsibility to steward those children God has given us. We model what it is to pray for our children before they ever come into this world. Do you see your children in their divine origin? They are cre-ated in the image of God. They are not accidents. They are not simply the result of two people coming together casually. Can you say, 'I prayed for this child'? Are you overwhelmed with the sacred privilege it is to give birth to a human being? Have you consecrated your little ones to the Lord before their birth and even before their conception? If you are a young person just starting out in life, I urge you to do so. Those of us who are older may have to do some retroactive praying.

Six, a godly parent *tries to have an understanding heart.*
A recent front-page article in the *Los Angeles Times* declared that freshmen in college, just beginning their collegiate odyssey, are far more stressed than those who have gone before. Quoting a nationwide survey, sponsored by UCLA's Higher Education Research Institute, which gathered responses from more than a quarter million freshmen, the article stated: 'More college fresh-men are stressed about money, their grades and getting ahead. More of them are smoking. More admit to being depressed, and a record number say they frequently "felt over-whelmed by all I have to do".'

We need to be increasingly understanding of the pressures our children and grandchildren face. We had our own problems growing up. Some of those, they'll never face – yet they face pressures that we've never known.

What an exciting privilege we have of finding creative ways to teach truth to our children from infancy on up and to model our own willingness to follow the Lord, to live by the teachings of Scripture, and to repent of our own sins, even as we try to provide responsible discipline for our children.

Seven, a godly parent *prays individually for their children.*
The other day I received a beautiful letter from a mother at our church. She writes:

> In a church this size, there needs to be more prayer support for the pastors, staff, interns, and student leaders who are trying to make a difference in the lives of young people. In our Moms In Touch group, there are only two moms ... coming together once a week to pray for our youth department. (We have changed the meeting time hoping to accommodate the schedules of others many times in the last four years.) Would you consider weaving into one of your sermons the importance of praying for our children, our youth department, and the schools? I think it is needful for our congregation to be reminded of the privilege and responsibility we, as parents and grandparents, have to pray for our children, grandchildren, and those who influence them.

Whether or not you join a group like this, remember to pray for your children and your grandchildren. They are special gifts from God. You have their personalities in your hands. You can shape, you can mold tender young lives.

A loving parent who daily intercedes on behalf of a child, bringing specific requests to the Lord, is making an investment for eternity. Several years ago, Anne shared with me what is a revolutionary thought. She said, 'Are you aware that the only possessions we now have which God has given to us and we can carry out of this life into heaven are our children?' I had never thought about it that way. We have a responsibility to consecrate them to the Lord in a spirit of gratitude and to pray that they will come to know Jesus Christ as Savior. Not only that. We have the privilege not of just introducing them to great literature, beautiful thoughts, redemption in Christ, but also to help them develop in lives of service for others, that they will be contributors to society.

Eight, godly parents *have respect for their child's individual autonomy.* What would be your reaction if one of your children would come to you, thumbing their nose at you, demanding that you give total freedom and a large chunk of money to finance their rebellion? That's a tough one, isn't it?

The story Jesus told about the Prodigal Son has taught me a lot about the importance of respecting my child's autonomy and how to treat each child as a unique person.

It was not unusual for a Jewish father to distribute his estate before he died if he wished to retire from the actual management of his business affairs. Under the law, there was a clear delineation of his financial responsibilities. The older son must get two-thirds and the younger son one-third. But there is a certain demanding attitude, is there not, on the part of this younger son? He is saying, 'Life is too short for me to wait for you to die or to retire. I am going to get it anyway. Give it to me now. I am bored. I am hemmed in. I want out!'

Remember, this was a parable. Jesus was creating the story as he told it. He didn't have to be faithful to historical events. He was trying to illustrate a point. He could have had the father say, 'No!' In that way, Jesus could have done some pretty good teaching about discipline and the setting of boundaries. Instead, Jesus shows a father who almost looks like a soft touch. This father didn't bludgeon his son in an authoritarian way. He didn't try to blackmail him, telling him how much more he would have in the long run if he would stay around home. He could have played the comparison game, saying, 'Why aren't you a good son like your older brother? What are you trying to do, break your mother's heart?' You know those games we play.

No, this father was prepared to stand by the teachings and the humble modeling that he and his wife had shared from their sons' infancy. He was willing to evaluate each one of them for who they were as individuals. He knew their strengths and weaknesses. He was prepared to let this young man be an adult. After all, he himself was human. He had had a father who raised him. He had had his own rivalries with his brothers and sisters. He knew the feeling of being compared. He knew what it was to want to be his own person. He knew what it was to rebel. We don't know the nature of his rebellion. We don't know much about his past. Perhaps he, at one time, had been the elder brother or some interesting blend of both of these personality types. He too had his secret sins as well as his more obvious shortcomings. He wasn't perfect. He knew that God, in his creative design, had not made human persons robots, automatons, which functioned as mechanical men and women. To be created human was to have the freedom to obey or to disobey. This model father had respect for the individual autonomy of each of his sons. So without preaching a doomsday sermon, he divided his estate, gave his son what he wanted, and bid him farewell.

That's tough to do. Just think of the trouble his son might get into. But it's important for us to do!

Nine, the godly parent *won't stand in the way of consequences for negative behavior.*

Apparently this father had money, and he had servants. He could have played a manipulative game. He could have assigned one of his servants to shadow the rebellious kid, wearing various disguises, going wherever he went, keeping an eye on him and then reporting back what was going on. He could have kept track of his associations so that he wouldn't squander the fortune, thinking, 'I've worked hard for all this money, and no son of mine is entitled to waste it'. If things got real bad, he could have brought him home, thinking, 'His mother and I could never live with ourselves if we knew our son was hanging out with prostitutes or catching a venereal disease or becoming an alcoholic or marrying outside of our faith'. At the first sting of homesickness, he could have had him reminded of his mother's hot chicken soup and the fact that there was always plenty of work and food at home.

The godly father, the godly mother won't stand in the way of consequences. Ours is not the business of premature rescue. As much as our hearts may be breaking and know that there is trouble ahead, we have to let go. Are we prepared to say, 'I love you. This is your life. I've done the best I can. It hasn't been all that good at some points. You know my weaknesses and my mistakes. Forgive me for them. This is your life. You know what I believe. I am willing to cut the strings of control. You are free to be who you choose to be, to do what you choose to do and to live with the consequences. You know I love you, and I always will.' With a big hug and perhaps a few tears, are we prepared to send them off to seek their own fortune, to face whatever may be the consequences – positive, negative, or in between?

Ten, a godly parent *is a celebrative person.*
Anne has had to teach me how to celebrate. It doesn't come easy for me. I am not much of a party person. My natural instinct, if a rebel child had come home, would be to sit down with a very-carefully-controlled, eye-to-eye, adult conversation, reflecting on the empirical realities of this unfortunate rebellion. I would declare myself as one willing to forgive but would be inclined to preach a sermon designed to preclude a repeat performance. My immediate instinct would not be to throw a party.

Jesus is teaching us how to celebrate restored relationship. At the deepest level, he is telling us about the nature of God who rejoices in our homecomings.

Eleven, a godly parent *is willing to live with ambiguity.*
We don't know the end of the story. We do know that the other son got angry. The father had to live with that anger. The other son viewed this as unfair. He wasn't the least bit interested in being part of the celebration.

It is interesting to see the different reactions of our children.

This father acknowledges the faithfulness of the older brother. He makes no demands for performance on the younger brother. Life goes on. None of us knows the future. Being a father, being a mother has no sealed and signed guarantees. We are called to live with the ambiguity that is built into relationships. The godly father, the godly mother accepts this as a fact of life and moves on, faithfully doing and being what God has called him or her to do and be – no matter what the significant others in their lives choose to do and be. Our final reward isn't the privilege of sitting back and saying, 'Wasn't I a good parent?' Granted, we'll have some joys that come from the hope for friendship with our children. But the final reward will be when the real Model, the Parent God, himself, looks us in the eyes and says, 'Well done, thou good and faithful servant. Enter into your eternal rest'.

Twelve, the godly parent *has a love that refuses to give up.*
The father in this story doesn't say, 'I told you so.' Nor does he minimize sinful behavior. Love explodes within him. He has compassion. He runs, embraces his son, kisses him. The son cries out, 'Father, I have sinned against heaven and against you. I am no longer worthy to be called your son' (Luke 15:21). The father doesn't linger even a minute over the son's acknowledged sinfulness and unworthiness. He shows a love and a forgiveness that refuses ever to give up.

Thirteen, the godly parent *knows that one of the best gifts a husband and wife can give to their children is for the husband and wife to love each other and to show it.*
Very little produces as much insecurity within children today than to be products of homes ripped apart by marital discord. Hannah and Elkanah could have benefitted from this insight. When Anne and I have not been loving to each other and our children have seen this, we have let them down. The flip side is that this love shouldn't be the sentimental, mushy denial of differences but a love that is so strong that it is prepared to confront the tough, hard realities of human existence. A child can be just as injured being raised in an environment that denies differences, where a husband and wife are so en-

meshed they almost seem to be one person. The best gift that we husbands and wives can give our children is to raise them in a loving environment, where we admit our own weaknesses and where the children are participants in the good times and in the tough times of our family odyssey.

It's a privilege to be this kind of a parent! Now, I am aware that I am not always one – nor are you. But the Parent understands we are not perfect. Because he loves and accepts us and never gives up. He models for us what it is to be there, in all of our own shortcomings and imperfections, for our children.

# CHAPTER 8
## HOW TO HANDLE YOUR PARENTS

*The eye that mocks a father, that scorns obedience to a mother, will be pecked out by the ravens of the valley, will be eaten by the vultures*

Proverbs 30:17

*Children, obey your parents in the Lord, for this is right. 'Honor your father and mother' — which is the first commandment with a promise — 'that it may go well with you and that you may enjoy long life on the earth'*

Ephesians 6:1-3

In the last two chapters, we've talked about parent-child relationships from the perspective of parents. Now we'll view the relationship from the vantage point of children – children of all ages.

Let me underline once again that I'm not writing this from the position of someone who has mastered these biblical teachings in his own life as a father or as a child. I'm wrestling with these issues along with you. God forbid that there be any attitude of arrogance or superiority. The starting point of everything I teach and preach is that the ground is level at the foot of the cross. None of us is perfect. That's another way of saying that all have sinned. Each of us, myself included, is part of the church, which could just as well be referred to as 'Sinners Anonymous'. This is a group of men and women of all ages who acknowledge that we are sinners and need the forgiveness, help, and strength of the Holy Spirit and each other to make it through one day at a time.

This leads me to some preliminary observations.

Observation one: *Adolescent rebellion, to some extent, is both healthy and normal.*

The teenager who acts like his parents, thinks like his parents, dresses like his parents, enjoys the same music his parents enjoy, is a unique character and may not be the healthiest of young people. There is a time to stretch. There is a time to differentiate and to see yourself as separate from mother and father. There is a time to think. There is a time to doubt your parents' entire lifestyle – philosophically, spiritually, and in practical matters of conduct. There is a time to move away from home. All of this is part of what we call adolescence. It must happen. The extent to which it happens and is encouraged within the healthy dynamics of the nuclear family, the better off both children and parents will end up being. Hopefully much of this coming of age can be worked out through the teenage years and the children then will rediscover their parents as friends.

If you are now about to graduate from college or if you are older than that, and if you are having deep struggles with your parents, you may very well be going through what is called postponed-adolescent rebellion. That may mean that you didn't go through the normal upheavals at the time when it is most healthy. In fact, I know some people who now, in their forties and fifties, are experiencing what they should have gone through earlier in life.

Observation two: *The Bible encourages loving confrontation.*

Loving confrontation is necessary if God's grace is to work. Ephesians 4:26 states that we are to express our anger in a way in which we sin not. Jesus was quite specific in Matthew, chapters 5 and 18, as to how we are to get together with our brother or sister in Christ with whom we have a difference and how to work out those differences. Even as husbands and wives are brothers and sisters in Christ, so are parents and children. Honest confrontation and love should be standard procedures in families.

For example, I discovered when our daughters were teen-agers that there is a considerable disparity between the music tastes of some parents and some teenagers. Going along with that, I discovered that usually one of the two parties prefers one volume setting, and the other prefers another. When one of those parties happens to be away at school in a dormitory where others share similar tastes in music and volume prefer-ences, there isn't any great problem. However, when that person comes back into their family environment and practices what is normal in another setting, the normalcy of this particular family is knocked off kilter. There had better be some substantial con-frontation and love that deals with the realities of two human beings, fine persons, created in the image of God, who, at least for a period of time, need to share the same space.

Another example. On many occasions I have made what I thought were marvelous plans for our family to do something together. But the response has been of such multitudinous, alternative viewpoints that I have begun to question whether I should ever again try to plan a family event. I have had to fight the tendency to retreat into my own little place of safety and never again reemerge. I would have been much better off to encourage a frank negotiation that deals with the realities of the individual needs of each family member before I had set out on my well-intentioned plan.

Issues of dress, standards, curfew, and many others must be dealt with honestly and in a straightforward manner.

Observation three: *Individual responsibility is one of the major themes that goes throughout the entire Bible.*
We live in a day in which we benefit from the psychological understanding that sees family problems as being intergen-erational, passed on from one generation to another. Actually, this is nothing new. There is substantial biblical basis for that conclusion.

However, there is also a biblical call for personal assump-tion of responsibility for one's own life and actions. With all the psychological insight we receive, we dare not relegate to others responsibility for our own actions if we are to function authentically as adults, exercising the God-given freedoms that are ours.

My thoughts keep being directed to Ezekiel 18 that brings these two dynamics into healthy tension. God quotes a proverb that perhaps had been misused by the people of Israel. He writes:

> The word of the Lord came to me: 'What do you people mean by quoting this proverb about the land of Israel:
> "The fathers eat sour grapes, and the children's teeth are set on edge?"
> 'As surely as I live,' declares the Sovereign Lord, 'you will no longer quote this proverb in Israel. For every living soul belongs to me, the father as well as the son – both alike belong to me. The soul who sins is the one who will die' (Ezek. 18:1-4).

He goes on to acknowledge that although there are family issues that move from one generation to another, God has given us freedom. He describes a man who lives in obedience to the law of God, who has a son who doesn't. The father is faithful to the decrees of God. Ezekiel gets very explicit in how that father was faithful. Then he goes on to describe how this man has a son who is violent, who sheds blood, and disobeys the teachings of God's Word, living a very different lifestyle. He declares the right of this young man to live a different lifestyle from his father's and to face the consequences of such actions. 'Will such a man live? He will not! Because he has done all these detestable things, he will surely be put to death and his blood will be on his own head' (Ezek. 18:13).

Then God tells how this second man has a son who sees the misguided ways of his father and how he, with the help of the Lord, lives according to the Word of God. God declares:

> He will not die for his father's sin; he will surely live. But his father will die for his own sin, because he practiced extor-

tion, robbed his brother and did what was wrong among his people (Ezek. 18:17-18).

Do you catch what is being said here? There are three generations. Even as there are influences that go from one generation to another, it is essential that you and I assume responsibility for who we are before God and not simply blame what we do wrong on the previous generation or walk around feeling guilty for that generation's sins.

Now let me get a bit more specific about this whole matter of handling hassles with your parents. Everybody has these hassles. You are not at all different if you experience problems with your parents. And these hassles are not limited to teenagers. They go on through adult years.

Recently I received a phone call from a young woman in her thirties who was troubled by a problem with her parents. That same day a businessman in his fifties was telling me about a problem he was having with his father who had done so much for him but was making demands on his family life.

Once again, I must underline the basic Christian truth. It is this: As long as you are a human being, subject to sin, living in a world of sinners, relating to parents who also are sinners, there will be problems. In fact, there is something wrong with your life if you have been exempt from child-parent difficulties. These hassles are normal.

However, you are not just a sinner. If you have accepted Jesus Christ as your personal Savior, you have the potential to move beyond bondage to these difficulties. Yours can be a liberating Christian maturity. The question is: How do we cope with child-parent trouble?

Some years back, a fourteen-year-old hit me point blank with the comment, 'My parents bug me! What can I do about them? They are impossible!'

You know something? Inwardly, I had to agree with her – although I couldn't tell her this. I knew her parents. They were impossible. They were bugging her. Her complaint was

legitimate. Her perceptions were reliable. What should I say?
Agree with her and leave it at that? No! My young friend had
missed the fact that she was part of this problem. Not only were
her parents giving her difficulty, she was making life impossible
for them. She had not learned some basic facts about her mom
and dad. It was only when she learned these that she was set
free to experience a much more exciting lifestyle.

Fact one she needed to know was this: *God created her parents
for her benefit.*

Can you grasp that fact? Your father and mother, as tough as
they are to understand at times, are God's gift to you. They are
part of an authority structure that helps you be the person God
wants you to be. In this world there is authority. God ordered
this authority. The Ten Commandments state: 'Honor your
father and mother.' The Apostle Paul, in the New Testament,
is led by the Holy Spirit to write:

> Children, obey your parents in the Lord, for this is right.
> 'Honor your father and mother' – which is the first com-
> mandment with a promise – 'that it may go well with you
> and that you may enjoy long life on the earth' (Eph. 6:1-3).

Do you catch the positive element of that command? You are
to obey. In the process, you will have a full, positive life. Paul
notes that this is the first commandment that gives a promise.
The promise is that if you obey, respecting the authority of your
parents, your lifestyle will be blessed of God. Whether this
is simply a psychological fact of life or whether God himself
goes out of his way to reward you is not clearly specified. I am
inclined to believe it is both, for the Bible is God's clear expression of how to live the life he created you to live.

On the other hand, the author of the Book of Proverbs warns
of what will happen if you don't take your parents seriously.
He states, 'The eye that mocks a father, that scorns obedience
to a mother, will be pecked out by the ravens of the valley, will
be eaten by the vultures' (Prov. 30:17). That's tough language,

isn't it? The person who disobeys the commands of God finds out that this actually happens. Your life is destroyed by your failure to live within God's authority structures.

What are these authority structures? The Bible teaches that God is able to accomplish his purpose in our lives through those he places in authority over us. In the family relationship this authority is entrusted to God and parents. Every teenager has an enormous potential for either beautiful living or chaotic ruin. In God's eyes, every child is a diamond in the rough. The father and mother serves along with God as master diamond cutters, working to bring out the finest qualities of the young person's God-given self. If you refuse to submit to the sometimes painful experience of being shaped by the authority of God and parents, you can end up realizing so little of your ultimate potential.

Fact two my young friend needed to know was this: *God instructs her to obey her parents – not to spoil her fun but because it's the intelligent way to live.*

God knows how you function best. He is the one who made you. Through his Word, he alerts you to a plan for living. He knows that your mother and father have insights that can be of enormous help. Why don't you try picking their brains?

I am speaking specifically now to teenagers, although we of all ages can continue to learn from our parents. As a teenager, you have your dating problems. You talk them over with your friends. Have you ever stopped to think that Mom and Dad can give you a lot of good advice? This is especially true if you are doing the asking. Remember, they were young once too. Remember, they've gone through the insecurities, frustrations, and problems that you are experiencing. Remember, they made some mistakes. Confront them with your questions. You'll be surprised at the wise answers they will give.

I realize that you may chuckle and say, 'I don't have to ask my parents. They're loaded with all kinds of advice without me even having to ask!' Why is that? Do you really want to know? It is because they really care.

Mom and Dad have a lot they can share with you. Sometimes even the worst parents have a God-given instinct as to what is best for their child.

I discovered this way back in my seminary days when I was serving at the Marble Collegiate Church in New York City. I was counseling a prostitute. She came with her five-year-old boy, Mike, who was born out of wedlock. This young woman was so mixed up. Yet she was determined that Michael would be free of the mistakes she had made in her teenage years. I will never forget the sincerity of this young woman who did not have her own act together but wanted what was best for her child.

You say, 'But I can't get my dad's time long enough to have a good talk. He is so busy in his work. And my mother, when she's not working, is at the gym or somewhere with her covenant group.'

Harold Mallett, a writer on family relationships, suggests writing a note to your parents. I'll guarantee it will catch their attention. He says to write something like this:

Dear Folks,

Do you mind if I make a suggestion? We don't talk enough. I realize how much 'Go' and 'Do' there is in your lives, and I know it's important. But frankly, I need some of your time. It's not that I'm in a jam, or intend to be, but somehow it seems that we belong to different denominations! I go my way and you go yours. We get along fairly well, but I'm like a roomer.

I'd like to discuss dating with you, and some problems that come up about school, parties, drinking, and such. I really need to know what you would say and do.

Could we agree on a time, soon, to fix other times when we can 'get with it' more? Yours for the talking!

Your parents were created for your benefit. Obey them because God tells you to and because God knows what is smart. You will be a lot happier this way.

You ask, 'Is there anything in which God allows me to diso-bey my parents?'

Yes, there is. I would be totally dishonest if I pretended that the Bible leaves you forever in bondage to your mother and father. There are two contingencies that free you from their authority.

Contingency one: *You don't have to obey your parents when what they are demanding goes in direct opposition to the Word of God – the Bible.*

Jesus said, 'Anyone who loves his father or mother more than me is not worthy of me ...' (Matt. 10:37).

God is the ultimate authority over your life. Jesus Christ should be first. You are free to disobey your parents when they force you to do something that goes against the Lord.

For example, there are some fathers and mothers whose lives are so perverted by sin that they enlist their child's aid in illegal activities. I know parents who have urged their children to lie and to steal.

Increasingly, we are hearing more stories of young people whose parents have used them sexually. God never expects you to obey your parents when they go against God's instructions for creative Christian living. Remember, though, you are going to have to know the Bible. You should be growing in your rela-tionship with the Lord so you know what is right and what is wrong. I believe, in most cases, the requests of parents do not go counter to the Word of God. But when they do, the highest authority is God, not Mom and Dad.

Please don't use this as a cop-out. Use this responsibly. In most cases, your commitment to the Lord will only increase the quality of your relationship with your parents as you, in a healthy way, acknowledge their authority.

Contingency two: *You don't have to obey your parents forever.* The day comes when you leave your father and mother.

If you are a single young adult, you will have the privilege and the responsibility of making your own decisions.

If you are married, the Bible urges you to leave your father and mother and to cleave to your partner.

As an adult, you will be primarily under the authority of God and his Word. Maturity in a young person means that you are able to develop in your relationship to God and your fellow human beings so that you are able to live as a responsible adult.

As long as you are dependent on your father and mother for money, you've got a responsibility to them.

One teenager I know has many hang-ups with his father. He went away to college. He and his dad continued to get along like cat and dog. It all boiled down to the fact that my friend wanted freedom from his dad. Yet he was content to have his father pay all of his expenses. When Dad made a request, he resented it. He was in bondage. Physically, he was an adult. Financially, he was a dependent. He wanted his freedom from everything except financial support. In the process, the bond was still tied tight. You are not ready for full freedom until you are no longer dependent upon your parents for financial support.

Up to this point, what I've shared is primarily for teenagers. You are probably responding, 'But I am an adult. Yet I still have problems with my parents.'

Certainly you do. As long as your parents are alive, they are part of your life. They provide enormous joy. At the same time, there is hurt.

There are three specific problems I see adult children face.

Problem one: *Possessive parents.*
So often I've heard this refrain: 'My parents are so possessive. They try to dictate my life.' I've heard this complaint from people in their twenties, thirties, and forties.

One friend went through thirty years of professional life hounded by his father in a business.

I know of another man in his forties with a lively brood of teenage children who is taking direct instructions from his parents, resenting it all the time. His mother has gone so far as to dictate where he lives and who his friends should be. He is being torn apart inside.

Frankly, this happens because the child doesn't have the sense to really leave home when he becomes an adult. He may get married. She may live thousands of miles away from her father and mother. At the same time, they have left a link of vital connection that keeps them in bondage. In most cases, that link is money. Most adults have problems with their parents because the parent-child ties never mature to the point of adult-to-adult friendship – usually because of a financial deal they've made with their parents.

If I am dependent upon my father for the home in which I live, the job which is mine, and the inheritance which will someday come, I will find myself involved in a love-hate relationship. I will love him because he is my father; I will hate him because my relationship with him is distorted. I am still a teenager dependent upon him instead of an adult who is self-sufficient, self-governing. Nothing is more pathetic than an adult who is dependent upon his parents for financial and emotional support. If you are caught up in that situation, get out of it. Allow your parent to be free, and allow yourself to be free. Or negotiate some kind of an understanding whereby you have clear boundaries.

Problem two: *In-laws.*
One psychologist states that 40 percent of the problems during early years of marriage are related to in-law difficulties. She says there are two major causes of this. One is when the parents do not emotionally release their child. Two is when the child does not emotionally break away from the parents. This child-parent problem becomes extremely complicated because it involves someone else's parents. There is a strange phenomenon that I have detected in counseling and in my own marriage. It is easy for your wife to criticize her own parents. She can make a list of her mother's weaknesses and her dad's weaknesses. But if you begin to list those weaknesses, you are in trouble. Why? Because you have criticized her when you thought you were criticizing her parents. She is a product of the people whom

you are criticizing. She expresses her independence when she analyzes them. You put her down when you analyze her.

The smart in-law is one who gives complete freedom to her sons or daughters to establish their own life with their new family. This means no financial support. Or if there is some financial help, such as a down payment on a home, make certain that there is a clear understanding of the implications.

The smart young couple is one that realizes that no set of in-laws is perfect. His parents are people; her parents are people. They love their son; they love their daughter. I believe you can best accept that love if you are free to let it be known that the two of you are primarily committed to each other. You have left your parents to make a husband-wife commitment. In turn, you are going to be loving to the parents of both – yet independent of them. This independence may require that you make material sacrifices in order to achieve complete emotional freedom.

Problem three: *Aging parents.*
I am spending an increased amount of my time in pastoral conversation with children in their fifties, sixties, and seventies as they are endeavoring to cope with the issues facing their aging parents who are now well into their eighties and nineties.

I am close to one couple in their seventies who have spent a major amount of their time since their retirement providing support for his aging mother and her aging father. The roles have changed. The care receivers have become the caregivers. The question now is how to establish firm boundaries that guarantee responsible support for one's parents yet the capacity to continue to live one's life meeting other responsibilities that also are important.

At any stage in life, the child-parent relationship is fraught with potential problems. There are the hassles. At the same time, the work we put into maintaining healthy relationships with those who brought us into the world is well worth it. The day will come when they are no longer with us.

My friend Joe found this out. During his twenties, thirties, and forties, he turned on his mother in revenge for her domination of his adolescence. He belittled her. He ridiculed her lifestyle. He talked about her behind her back. Then she died. Joe couldn't accept her death. Burdened with guilt, he went into severe depression. The mere mention of her name brought tears to his eyes. He had abused a special trust relationship. It was only when he accepted God's forgiveness in Christ that he was set free from his bondage. Still, he longs to have her back again to express his love and appreciation. He'll never be able to do it in this life. He let his hassles with his mother get the better of him in a way which clouds his life.

I came across this bit of whimsy that describes this fascinating child-parent odyssey. It is titled 'Father'.

4 Years: My daddy can do anything.
7 Years: My dad knows a lot, a whole lot.
8 Years: My father doesn't quite know everything.
12 Years: Oh well, naturally Father doesn't know everything.
14 Years: Father? Hopelessly old-fashioned.
21 Years: Oh, that man is out of date. What did you expect?
25 Years: He knows a little bit about it but not much.
30 Years: Must find out what Dad thinks about it.
35 Years: A little patience. Let's get Dad's thoughts first.
50 Years: What would Dad have thought about it?
60 Years: My dad knew literally everything.
65 Years: I wish I could talk it over with Dad once more.

I don't know where you are in this child-parent odyssey. Perhaps now is the time, before it's too late, to pick up the phone or to write a letter and say, 'I am sorry'. Or perhaps all you need to do is reestablish or maintain communication in the way that takes your parents seriously as God's personal gift to you.

If it has been a troubled relationship, one with abuse, you may just have to keep those boundary lines clear. Talk to the

Lord about those issues and get therapy if you continue to be troubled. Hopefully you will come to the day when you will forgive your father and/or your mother for the mistakes they made – even if they are incapable of understanding the full degree of those mistakes.

Hopefully you can identify the wonderful qualities in your parents and take the initiative now to express your appreciation to them. If they are not alive, thank God for his gift of parents!

# CHAPTER 9
## WHY JESUS DOESN'T LIKE DIVORCE

*'It was because your hearts were hard that Moses wrote you this law,' Jesus replied. 'But at the beginning of creation God "made them male and female". 'For this reason a man will leave his father and mother and be united to his wife, and the two will become one flesh.' So they are no longer two, but one. Therefore what God has joined together, let man not separate'*

Mark 10:5-9

Although I have preached and written often about marriage, I would just as soon not talk about divorce. It is one of the most painful topics one can address in contemporary America. Is there one of us who has not been touched by it in some painful manner?

If you and I have not actually experienced our own divorce, at least we have vicariously walked through that tearing-apart experience with a loved one.

In my childhood days divorce was very much the exception instead of the norm. I knew very few Christian couples who were divorced. Obviously, that has changed.

The Religion News Service recently carried a story in which the opening paragraph reads:

Although traditional Christian teaching rejects divorce and stresses marital fidelity and family values are central to the religious conservatives' moral agenda, recent data shows divorce strikes born-again Christians at about the same rate as those who don't profess a born-again experience.

The article goes on to note that the Barna Research Group, a California-based polling and marketing organization that specializes in religion, even found that those who characterize themselves as 'fundamentalists' have a slightly higher divorce rate than the general public.

The data showing that Christians were no more immune to divorce than the general population disturbed Tom Whiteman, a Philadelphia psychologist and counselor. He focused on this matter in his doctoral research. He found that even though devout Christians divorce at about the same rate as others, they did so for different reasons. Whereas the number one reason cited for divorce in the general population was incompatibility, Christians rarely use that as grounds for divorce. In the Christian population, the primary reasons are adultery, abuse (including substance, physical and verbal abuse) and abandonment. In fact, Christians tend to hang on to bad marriages longer than others do.

> 'The good news is that we are staying together longer and taking marriage seriously, but the bad news is we're putting up with a lot more pain, and ending up getting divorced anyway.'

One might conclude from this data that Christians are worse than nonbelievers at picking partners. I am inclined to conclude that we are not as quick to accept the label 'incompatibility' as an easy way out. We are willing to put up with a lot more pain as we endeavor to try to make a difficult marriage work.

Although divorce is more frequent than ever before, it certainly is not a new topic. In fact, divorce was as painful a matter in the time of Jesus as it is today.

One day, the Pharisees were determined to trick Jesus with one of their loaded questions. They asked, 'is it lawful for a man to divorce his wife?' (Mark 10:2). Mark tells us that the Pharisees came and tested Jesus – not with an honest question but with one designed to do him evil. They were probing for his vulnerable point. They were trying to either cause him to sin against God in a way that would publicly repudiate the moral force of his teaching or, with clever sophistry, to trick him into some embarrassing statement that would facilitate their goal of putting him to death.

Their question about divorce was a no-win topic for Jesus. There was no way he could answer their question without alienating someone. If he opposed divorce on legal grounds, he would end up contradicting the Law of Moses. If he opposed it on moral grounds, he exposed himself to the same fate as John the Baptist, who, at the hands of the adulterer Herod Antipas, was beheaded. At the same time, if he accepted divorce on legal grounds, he subjected the rest of his teaching to the Law of Moses and the very constricted interpretation that the Pharisees gave to that law.

One thing that Jewish scholars could do very well was haggle over biblical interpretation. In Deuteronomy 24:1 Moses declared that a man could divorce his wife if he found out something 'indecent' about her.

For one school of rabbis, followers of Shammai, that was interpreted with the utmost strictness. The matter of uncleanness was adultery, and that alone. She could be guilty of many other sins but unless there was actual sexual adultery that could be proven, there could be no divorce.

At the other extreme was the school of Hillel. These scholars gave the most liberal interpretation possible to the teaching of Moses. They went so far as to say that if she spoiled a dish of food, if she talked to a strange man, if she spoke disrespectfully of her in-laws, if her voice was too loud, or if her husband happen to find a more attractive woman, he could get rid of her. Divorce was permissible for the most trivial reasons. In the time of Jesus, as it is today, this was tragically common. Some women in the Jewish community hesitated to marry at all because the institution of marriage was so insecure. Jesus, by giving the answers which he gave, 'Therefore what God has joined together, let man not separate' (Mark 10:9), not only was dealing with a first-century epidemic of divorce, he was also protecting the rights of women who were so often treated as objects to be owned and then discarded by their husbands.

In a way, circumstances of his day were not that different from now – except that now women are as quick to divorce men as men are to divorce women.

I had to wrestle intensely with this matter of divorce when in 1981 we called Bill Flanagan to join our pastoral staff at St. Andrew's Presbyterian Church. He already had developed a successful singles ministry at the First Presbyterian Church in Colorado Springs, Colorado. Part of that ministry involved what we now know as the 'Divorce Recovery Workshop'. Flan frankly told me that addressing this issue within the context of the church and the welcoming of divorced people into the programs of St. Andrew's could upset some people. And it did. Over these past two decades we have had well over 13,000 divorced persons and their children who go through our twice-a-year, six-Thursday-nights-in-a-row Divorce Recovery Workshop. There have been some who have felt that we have been too accepting of divorce. On the other hand, because we make frequent mention of the pain accompanying divorce and speak out against divorce as too frequently used as a way out of difficulty, there are some who feel that we are too strict.

I know that this topic is threatening to some at this very moment because they are divorced. Perhaps you are divorced. You have worked through your pain. The last thing you need from me is to be made to feel guilty about this event, which is now part of your past. On the other hand, there is someone right now dealing with tough stuff in his or her marriage. You may be one of these, and you need to hear what Jesus has to say about divorce.

Although Jesus doesn't have a whole lot to say about divorce, on those few occasions that he addressed this topic what he did say was extremely sensitive to human pain and also very strong in the warning that he gives.

*First,* Jesus declares a *realistic* word.

He shares with us the legal protections designed in the Law of Moses. He did this by responding to the trick questions of the religious leaders with a question of his own. He asked, 'What did Moses command you?' (Mark 10:3). Knowing that Moses had made provision for divorce, He readily anticipated their response. 'Moses permitted a man to write a certificate of divorce and send her away' (Mark 10:4).

At this point, Jesus notes why Moses allowed for this. He seems to underscore the word 'permitted', which implies this was not the most ideal reality. Divorce was something that was designed to deal with human aberration. In essence, the permission Moses gave for divorce served, then and now, as an indictment of the human condition. Moses had hoped, at best, that this legislation would prove to be temporary in nature and would be ruled irrelevant by a spiritual revival among the Jews, who would once again put the spirit of love above the letter of the Jewish law. Nonetheless, he was not prepared for spouses to stay in marriages that were abusive and destructive.

Jesus responded to the trick question of the Pharisees by declaring that divorce was not God's standard, that Moses allowed divorce because of the hardness of human hearts. Moses didn't command divorce. He simply permitted it for the protection of women so that they would not be subject to exploitation and vindictiveness. Or to put it another way, divorce was a divine concession to human weakness and acknowledgment of humankind's sinfulness. Moses, Jesus, and Paul never encouraged divorce. At the very best, it was a reluctant permission.

*Second,* Jesus gives a *spiritual* word.

Jesus is saying, God hates divorce. God never intended for male-female relationship to be ripped apart. Jesus states, 'It was because your hearts were hard that Moses wrote you this law' (Mark 10:5).

Then Jesus added these most telling words:

'But at the beginning of creation God "made them male and female". 'For this reason a man will leave his father and mother and be united to his wife, and the two will become one flesh.' So they are no longer two but one. Therefore, what God has joined together, let not man separate' (Mark 10:6-9).

I have been struggling to find a way to somehow get across to all of us that proper combination between the realism in which Jesus declares there is the necessity in certain cases for divorce but, on the other hand at a much deeper and profound level, get across the dreams that God has for those of us who are married. I won't be successful by a clever juxtaposition of human words that makes those of you who have gone through the brokenness of divorce feel good about it and makes those who have not yet been divorced motivated to hang in there and make your marriage work. I certainly am not here to try to make you feel guilty if you've gone through the tragedy of divorce or to intimidate you into staying married in what may very well be a tragically abusive relationship.

What I would like to do is shift gears and simply quote to you some statements that come out of contemporary life that I believe pretty well illustrate what Jesus was trying to get across.

I have more than 20 huge file drawers in my study filled with manila folders into which I have, over the past 38 years, placed materials I have gathered by topic. One of these thick folders is labeled 'Divorce'. And the other is labeled 'Marriage'. Both are stuffed full of material.

Let me share some excerpts with you.

John Adam and Nancy Williamson, in their book, *Divorce: How and When to Let Go*, wrote:

Your marriage can wear out. People change their values and lifestyles. People want to experience new things. Change is a part of life. Change and personal growth are traits for you to be proud of, indicative of a vital searching mind. You must accept the reality that in today's multifaceted world it is especially easy for two persons to grow apart. Letting go of your marriage if it is no longer fulfilling can be the most successful thing you have ever done. Getting a divorce can be a positive, problem-solving, growth-oriented step. It can be a personal triumph.

Does this sound familiar? Is this not the spirit of our day? A friend of mine, Kent Hughes, writes:

> What an amazing thing. By making self-fulfillment the guiding principle of life, one can call *failure* 'success', *disintegration* 'growth', and *disaster* 'triumph'.

The human mind is capable of immense perversity. How often those of us who are pastors have been confronted by persons who have used this rationale to walk out on a marriage of many years.

I think of someone right now who has worked so hard to convince me of the rightness of his divorce. He walked out on his wife, who had sacrificed her own education so she could work to pay his way through graduate school. She gave up her own possible professional advancement to stay home and raise their children. This was his wish. After twenty-plus years of this, he began to complain that she wasn't as interesting as he'd like her to be. She didn't have an education to match his. He found her boring. Other women could carry on much more stimulating conversations. He complained about her appearance, and he moved out on her and in with a woman fifteen years younger, trying to convince both his wife and me, his pastor, that he was really doing her and the children a favor. How sad! How sickening! Her dreams had been shattered. The kids were dizzied, their lives, at the best, distorted, and, at the worst, partially destroyed by this family fracture.

I know a woman, and you know someone like her also, who, after a couple of decades of marriage and three children, is looking for more out of life than her husband offers. She aims a lot of blame at him for not being 'sensitive enough', and she talks a lot about, 'I have to be me. After all, self-actualization is what it's all about'. You know the rest of the story.

If you came over to St. Andrew's Presbyterian Church on Thursday nights and looked in on the Divorce Recovery Workshop, you'll see hundreds of men and women experiencing the pain and brokenness of commitments and hopes smashed. They are in the process of healing from broken dreams.

For close to four decades I have been officiating at weddings. I have done the premarital counseling and married several hundred couples. I have never yet met a couple who, when they came to the altar, didn't dream about spending the rest of their lives together. I must admit, in the last decade or so, I have done premarital counseling for couples who, because of what they observed of the shattered dreams of other couples, are a bit gun-shy of marriage. Every one of them will honestly express their deep desire for a commitment and relationship that will last "til death doth part'.

God didn't create marriage for divorce. He had something better in mind. Whether it's as heart-breakingly selfish as 'my right to be me' or something at the other extreme as devastatingly catastrophic as spousal abuse, divorce wasn't God's dream and plan for that couple. He allows it because of the hardness of heart of one or two people who are not willing to make those major adjustments that will produce health within the marriage relationship.

Let me quote to you from a secular book titled *Death of a Marriage* by Pat Conroy. You may be familiar with his novels. If you are contemplating a divorce and you have been asking the Lord for guidance, perhaps his honest statement will help you confront what's ahead.

Conroy writes:

> Each divorce is the death of a small civilization. Two people declare war on each other, and their screams and tears infect their entire world with the bacilli of their pain. The greatest fury comes from the wound where love once issued forth.

I find it hard to believe how many people now get divorced, how many submit to such extraordinary pain. For there are no clean divorces. Divorces should be conducted in surgical wards. In my own case, I think it would have been easier if Barbara had died. I would have been gallant at her funeral and shed real tears – far easier than staring across a table, telling each other it was over.

It was a killing thing to look at the mother of my children and know that we would not be together for the rest of our lives. It was terrifying to say goodbye, to reject a part of my own history.

When I went through my divorce I saw it as a country, and it was treeless, airless; there were no furloughs and no holidays. I entered without passport, without directions and absolutely alone. Insanity and hopelessness grew in that land like vast orchards of malignant fruit. I do not know the precise day that I arrived in that country. Nor am I certain that you can ever renounce your citizenship there.

Each divorce has its own metaphors that grow out of the dying marriage. One man was inordinately proud of his aquarium. He left his wife two weeks after the birth of their son. What visitors noticed next was that she was not taking care of the aquarium. The fish began dying. The two endings became linked in my mind.

For a long time I could not discover my own metaphor of loss – until the death of our dog, Beau, who became the irrefutable message that Barbara and I were finished.

Beau was a feisty, crotchety dachshund Barbara had owned when we married. It took a year of pained toleration for us to form our alliance. But Beau had one of those illuminating inner lives that only lovers of dogs can understand. He had a genius for companionship. To be licked by Beau when you awoke in the morning was a fine thing.

On one of the first days of our separation, when I went to the house to get some clothes, my youngest daughter, Megan, ran out to tell me that Beau had been hit by a car and taken to the animal clinic. I raced there and found Ruth

Tyree, Beau's veterinarian. She carried Beau in to see me and laid him on the examining table.

I had not cried during the terrible breaking away from Barbara. I had told her I was angry at my inability to cry. Now I came apart completely. It was not weeping; it was screaming; it was despair.

The car had crushed Beau's spine, the X-ray showing irreparable damage. Beau looked up at me while Dr. Tyree handed me a piece of paper, saying that she needed my signature to put Beau to sleep.

I could not write my name because I could not see the paper. I leaned against the examining table and cried as I had never cried in my life, crying not just for Beau but for Barbara, the children, myself, for the death of a marriage, for inconsolable loss. Dr. Tyree touched me gently, and I heard her crying above me. And Beau, in the last grand gesture of his life, dragged himself the length of the table on his two good legs and began licking the tears as they ran down my face.

I had lost my dog and found my metaphor. In the X-ray of my dog's crushed spine, I was looking at a portrait of my broken marriage.

But there are no metaphors powerful enough to describe the moment when you tell the children about the divorce. Divorces without children are minor-league divorces. To look into the eyes of your children and to tell them that you are mutilating their family and changing all their tomorrows is an act of desperate courage that I never want to repeat. It is also their parents' last act of solidarity and the absolute sign that the marriage is over. It felt as though I had doused my entire family with gasoline and struck a match.

The three girls entered the room and would not look at me or Barbara. Their faces, all dark wings and grief and human hurt, told me that they already knew. My betrayal of these young, sweet girls filled the room.

They wrote me notes of farewell, since it was I who was moving out. When I read them, I did not see how I could ever survive such excruciating pain. The notes said, 'I love you,

Daddy. I will visit you.' For months I would dream of visiting my three daughters locked in a mental hospital. The fear of damaged children was my most crippling obsession.

For a year I walked around feeling as if I had undergone a lobotomy. There were records I could not listen to because of their association with Barbara, poems I could not read from books I could not pick up. There is a restaurant I will never return to because it was the scene of an angry argument between us. It was a year when memory was an acid.

I began to develop the odd habits of the very lonely. I turned the stereo on as soon as I entered my apartment. I drank to the point of not caring. I cooked elaborate meals for myself, then could not eat them.

I had entered into the dark country of divorce, and for a year I was one of its ruined citizens. I suffered. I survived. I studied myself on the edge, and introduced myself to the stranger who lived within.

Barbara and I had one success in our divorce, and it is an extraordinarily rare one. As the residue of anger and hurt subsided with time, we remained friends. We saw each other for lunch occasionally, and I met her boyfriend, Tom.

Once, when I was leaving a party, I looked back and saw Barbara and Tom holding hands. They looked very happy together, and it was painful to recognize it. I wanted to go back and say something to Tom, but I mostly wanted to say it to Barbara. I wanted to say that I admired Tom's taste in women.

Wow, isn't that amazing? That's as graphic a description as I have ever read. It's what I as a pastor hear time and time again in the intimacy of my counseling ministry!

Another clipping in my file is titled *Children Suffer Financially From Divorce*. Two hundred families going through divorce were tracked for three years in the mid-1980s. The families were selected at random and reflected the U.S. population in every way, including income level, location, and race. It was the broadest study of its kind, taken from materials made available by the

Census Bureau. The conclusion is that children can expect to become 37 percent poorer almost as soon as their families breakup.

Once parents separate, fewer than half the children surveyed receive child support, further impoverishing them, the study said. The study's trends held true regardless of race and income level.

Other findings of the census report include:

The percentage of children living in poverty increased from 19 percent of the total to 36 percent immediately after the family split up. The number of children in families receiving Aid to Families with Dependent Children doubled after a divorce, from 9 percent to 18 percent. The number of children receiving food stamps increased from 10 percent before divorce to 27 percent after divorce.

Judith Wallerstein's and Sandra Blakeslee's exhaustive study of children in broken families, *Second Chances: Men, Women and Children, a Decade After Divorce*, assesses the carnage that litters North America's matrimonial battlefields, producing children who are part of a lost generation. This study notes that although initially it is the older children who appear to be least affected by the divorce, the long-term impact on them is just as severe, if not more so, than that upon the younger children.

Barbara Dafoe Whitehead has written a book titled *The Divorce Culture*. In it she laments the impact of divorce on children and the open wound that continues to fester. She notes the economic hardship that comes from divorce and declares that fatherless children could perhaps put up with economic difficulty if it weren't for the appalling psychological fallout that comes from their parents' breakup. She says that even the death of a parent is less traumatic. At least death is final. Divorce is an open wound that continues to fester. Death is usually involuntary; whereas divorce is voluntary on the part of at least one parent – a distinction that is not lost on children. Whitehead calls for Americans to recover 'vision of the obligated self, voluntarily bound to a set of roles, duties, and responsibilities and of a nation where sacrifice for the next generation guides adult ambitions and purposes'.

I believe one of the most heart-breaking items I have in my file is a letter written by a young woman who grew up at St. Andrew's. She wrote this for her class at Newport Harbor High School. I was so touched by it that I received permission not only from her, but also from her mother and father to use it. Its contents are painful! Read it carefully, for this is what I, as a pastor, hear and feel from the children of divorce. It is titled *Torn in Two* and is written to her father.

> My tears of sorrow are nothing new
> Because there are two sides to you:
> The love of which I am a part,
> And the hate which breaks my tender heart.
>
> Although I sob in deep despair.
> For I miss the father that I once knew
> Before my life was torn in two....
>
> He used to be so loving and kind.
> Now hate and deception inhabit his mind.
> What did I do to deserve such a change?
> For now our relationship must rearrange.
>
> His caring ways fade quickly away,
> As childish threats come into play.
> Whatever happened to being good friends?
> Then fly by many fatherless weekends.
>
> While claiming that Christ is part of his life,
> He discards his daughters and his Ex-wife.
> Instead of sending any child support,
> He mails a summons to see us in court.
>
> I know both sides of this pitiful tale,
> So must we dwell on each petty detail?

I know things can't be the way that they were,
But you'll always and forever be my father.

Whenever we speak about matters of money,
He says, 'You shouldn't even know about that, honey'.
But how could I not when each debt and loan
Contributed to the loss of our home.

Perhaps my heart could take to mending,
But his quest for revenge seems never ending.
Revenge against the woman for whom he once cared;
The one with whom two daughters he shared.

I hope that someday our quarrels will end.
And we'll find in each other a life-long friend.
Will you ever open your heart and let the good shine
through?
Or will I always feel as if I'm torn in two?

This is tough stuff, isn't it? I know no better way to capture
what Jesus was trying to say. This was not what God had in
mind when he created man and woman and entrusted them to
each other. God has dreams for you and me as to what marriage
can be for a man and a woman and for their children.

*Third*, Jesus has a *warning* word.
It's a tough word for those who don't take their vows seriously
and who initiate a marital breakup. He has declared that God's
purpose for marriage has not changed. A contemporary provision which Moses gave for divorce is not God's norm. It is only
the proof of human sin. Jesus could have made an angry attack
on divorce. Instead he endeavored to elevate the sacredness of
marriage. As David McKenna, for so many years the president
of Asbury Theological Seminary, has so insightfully observed, a
man is to break away from his parents and be joined to his wife
so that '1 + 1 = 1' in their relationship. Yoked together in the presence of God, this relationship of husband and wife is permanent.

Jesus has not intended to dodge the question put to him by the Pharisees. Instead, by their own scriptures, they must admit God's original intention for marriage has not changed.

Later on, when Jesus and his disciples are alone in the house, the conversation continues. They are still confused about divorce. If what Jesus said publicly is taken literally, divorce is not permissible under any circumstances. His response now can be quite confusing. He says, 'Anyone who divorces his wife and marries another woman commits adultery against her. And if she divorces her husband and marries another man, she commits adultery' (Mark 10:11-12).

That's a strong warning. No, Jesus is not endeavoring to introduce a new legalism to produce twenty-first-century Pharisees. At the same time, he refuses to back away from the truth that divorce is a symptom of sin and that permanence in marriage is God's intention. Take this in the context of Matthew's account. He quotes Jesus as saying, 'Moses permitted you to divorce your wives because your hearts were hard. But it was not this way from the beginning. I tell you that anyone who divorces his wife, except for marital unfaithfulness, and marries another woman commits adultery' (Matt. 19:8-9).

He's just saying, there's something more important than our own self-fulfillment and our own happiness. It is obedience to God's Word. This word 'unfaithfulness' comes from the Greek work *porneia*, from which we get the English word pornography. It means unchastity, fornication, prostitution, and other kinds of unlawful intercourse. When applied to married persons it becomes 'marital unfaithfulness'. It may involve adultery, homosexuality, bestiality, and other abusive distortions of our sexuality. It is the only grounds on which Jesus permitted divorce and remarriage. Even under these circumstances he didn't command divorce. He only permitted it. Even then it is not to be used simply as an excuse to get out of a marriage. The fact is that God's heart is broken by any and all perverted relationships. What he most yearns for is transformation of relational healing as both persons are open to the health-giving work of the Holy Spirit.

The apostle Paul elaborated slightly on this in 1 Corinthians 7:8-16. He spoke to a situation that Jesus did not address, that of believing spouses married to unbelieving partners. He urges the believing spouse to remain faithful to the marriage, yet not to force the non-believing spouse to stay in the marriage. Even as he acknowledges that unfortunately there may be divorce, it is preferable for the two to remain together with the believing spouse having a sanctifying influence on both the marriage and the family.

Let me give this final word that summarizes the whole tone of the New Testament teaching about marriage and divorce. We simply must, as Christians, live lives that run counter to this crazy, superficial, soap-opera culture in which we live. Commitment to a godly life does not guarantee that a marriage will work. But God does know how you and I function best. Our marriages can derive a deepening and a strength if we allow him to help us.

We must offer God's grace to others and ourselves. Wherein circumstances have escalated beyond what we know is God's intention and divorce has become a reality, God still loves us. The Gospel is Good News. Christ's grace is sufficient for us. He wants to help wipe away the tears and bring healing, wholeness, and new beginning, empowered by his Holy Spirit, which ministers tenderly and gently to us and our need and the needs of those injured by our brokenness! At the same time, those of us who still are blessed to be married have the privilege to encounter the tough realities of life lived in relationship with another person, claiming Christ's help to work through the tough stuff, which will enable our marriages to be much healthier and a blessing to our children.

# CHAPTER 10
## YOU CAN'T HAVE A PERFECT MARRIAGE —
## AND YOU WOULDN'T WANT ONE

*So they are no longer two, but one. Therefore what God has joined together, let man not separate*

Matthew 19:6

I hate divorce. You hate divorce. And God hates divorce.

At the same time, we have already seen that although God hates divorce he allows it to protect people from destroying themselves because of the hardness of the human heart.

Just because divorce is permitted does not mean that it is desirable. In the last chapter I spent a lot of time quoting people who have gone through the experience of divorce and who shared the pain of what that did to them, their spouse, and their children.

Divorce is not the answer. Divorce may be necessary in extreme situations. Moses, Jesus, and Paul acknowledged that fact – but we must be sobered by these words of Jesus: 'Moses permitted you to divorce your wives because your hearts were hard. But it was not this way from the beginning. I tell you that anyone who divorces his wife, except for marital unfaithfulness, and marries another woman commits adultery' (Matt. 19:8).

Let's take a realistic look at marriage. I'd like to make several observations.

Observation one: *There is no such thing as a perfect marriage.*
Does your marriage have problems? I hope so! Don't be so surprised when I say, 'I hope so!'

The fact is that there is no such thing as a perfect marriage. To have a perfect marriage you would have to have two perfect people. I know no one who can bear that label. There are various degrees of marriage – from horrible to quite good. Even the best marriage has its problems – because people have problems and marriages are made up of people.

Some of the couples with whom I share premarital counseling probably consider me a killjoy. I spend a lot of time talking about the fact that if two imperfect people marry, the result will be an imperfect marriage. That's a simple, realistic fact of life.

The average engaged couple has difficulty taking my comments seriously. Their eyes are aglow with love. They are enthusiastic about the forthcoming wedding. So often they comment to each other, 'Isn't it amazing how much we have in common, how we enjoy the same things, how much we think alike?' Life looks like that as two people gaze into each other's eyes, across a candlelit table. It's hard to picture that within a few short months after the marriage, if they would honestly admit their feelings, they might say something like this: 'Isn't it amazing how different we are, how unalike we think, how dissimilar our responses to life?'

One pastor I know has completely stopped premarital counseling. Instead he requires that each couple he plans to marry agree, prior to their wedding, to post-marital counseling. He has discovered that they are much more receptive to discussions after a few weeks of marriage than they would have been before the wedding.

Some face tough issues such as: spousal abuse; substance abuse; mental illness; gambling addiction; sexual addiction; and careerism. We cannot pretend that they don't exist.

Even if you do not confront anything as difficult as those, the healthiest couples face issues such as: differences in family backgrounds; problems with in-laws; financial matters; differences in religious backgrounds; differing temperaments; irritating habits; varying approaches to raising children; and the complex area of sex.

I have yet to meet a couple that has not had to confront these realities and come up with their own creative ways of coping with them. Some couples, simply by nature of their tempera-ment, find marital adjustment much easier than those who are temperamentally wired differently. Anne and I have discovered that the very qualities that drew us together, made us extremely attractive to each other – each have a flip side. Those same quali-ties can become irritants in changing circumstances.

For example, Anne and I are opposites in that she is a highly intuitive and quite impulsive person. I am quite methodical and almost compulsively organized. I was drawn to her by my deep need for someone who would provide spontaneity and excite-ment to my life. Anne has done just that. Sometimes she does too much of it in that I cannot always anticipate what she is thinking, and I find myself confused by her impulsivity, and irritated by the fact that what I anticipate happening seldom happens that way. She simply is not a conventional person. She, at times, finds great security in my organized predictability. At other times she is extremely frustrated by that same quality that throws a wet blanket on her creativity and can make me just plain boring.

Observation two: *Remember, there is a real difference between a man and a woman.*

One of my favorite musicals is *My Fair Lady*. I saw it several times on the London stage. Julie Andrews, then a teenager, was playing the role of Eliza Doolittle. Rex Harrison, playing the role of Professor Henry Higgins, was attempting to take the young, uncouth seller of flowers off the London streets and make her into a cultured person by teaching her the good manners of speech. This left-brained intellectual discovered it wasn't as easy as he thought it would be. The fact was that whatever her background, acculturation, and potential for change, he was caught off guard and totally perplexed by her feminine emotionality. What he thought he could accomplish, through a rational, academic approach, didn't happen. Finally, he threw up his hands in despair, singing out the question that we men have been singing all through human history, 'Why can't a woman be more like a man?'

Perhaps today that question should be reversed to query, 'Why can't a man be more like a woman?'

A careful study of psychology, sociology, and biblical truth will bear out the fact that males and females are designed to be complementary to each other. Therefore, they are different. Any man who thinks he can fully figure out a woman is kidding himself. Any woman who thinks she fully understands how a man is wired is going to be sadly disillusioned. We are different in design, even as we are equal in our humanity.

You add to that the reality of sin, as it has tainted us as humans, and you have a complex and discouraging setting for conflict and dysfunction.

We men and women need to hold each other accountable for our attitudes and behaviors while going out of our way to give each other some maneuvering room. It's important that we accept the fact that we are different and never will fully understand each other while, at the same time, working at being as understanding a partner as is possible.

Observation three: *Contentment is not a matter of circumstance but of attitude.*

God encourages you and me to cultivate a spirit of contentment. The Apostle Paul wrote these words of self-reflection:

> ... for I have learned to be content whatever the circumstances. I know what it is to be in need, and I know what it is to have plenty. I have learned the secret of being content in any and every situation, whether well fed or hungry, whether living in plenty or in want. I can do everything through him who gives me strength (Phil. 4:11-13).

This does not mean you and I are not to work at bettering our circumstances. We are free to change what we can change. However, there are some circumstances in life that one cannot change without creating even greater pain for one's self and for another. We are privileged to change those things that we can change and to claim God's serenity to live with those circumstances we cannot change. Our real contentment in life comes from our calling in Christ, not from some artificially induced change in our human circumstances. This has profound implications for marriage.

The point is that Jesus wants you and me to be his faithful followers just where we are. Some of us are so eager to break away from our jobs, from our circle of friends, even from our marriages. We think that if we could just get a fresh start in life we would have greater contentment. We think a change in our circumstances will solve our problems. Actually, God may want us to bloom right here where he has already planted us. We have to be careful not to keep wanting what we don't have, wanting to do what we can't do. We can improve ourselves in whatever ways self-improvement is possible, but we need to remember that our human status is not the final determination of who we really are. The fact that we have come to faith in Jesus Christ makes us sons and daughters of the living God. No one, not even a marriage partner, can take that away from us. What a privilege we have in realizing God's gift of grace and the enormous potential he has given us to be content in whatever circumstances we find ourselves.

I know people today who have everything and are not happy. I know people today who have very little and experience wholeness of life in Jesus Christ. I see it in my own life and experience. There have been moments this week in which I have allowed myself the slavery of negative attitudes, of self-pity, of fear, of resentment, that have left me immobilized. I have blamed the circumstances, allowing them to shape my attitude. And there have been moments this week when I have reminded myself of what it is to be set free by the grace of the Lord Jesus Christ. In those moments in which I remind myself of his transformational grace, I rise above my circumstances, which have not changed, to a sense of the peace of God that passes all understanding.

I've discovered, the longer I'm married and the more I grow in my relationship with both Anne and Jesus Christ, it is easier for me to find this state of contentment. But the reality is, God is not finished with me yet. Nor have I arrived. I've got a lot more growing to do!

Through the years, I've observed many marriages, as have you. I have seen some in which a partner is always upwardly mobile – wanting more from their spouse and even leaving the marriage for someone 'better'. And I've seen marriages in which a partner may have very good reason to leave the marriage from a human perspective but has chosen to keep the marriage commitment under the most difficult and complex of circumstances.

I think now of one man who has literally put his own career on hold to stand by a wife who struggles with enormous emotional and physical illness.

I think now of a woman who was raised in affluence who is standing by her husband who has had substantial financial reversals, willing to go to work to help supplement the family income and provide materially for their children.

Even as I make a mental list of these couples who have learned that their contentment is not a matter of circumstances but of attitude, I can list for you others who live in restless discontent – always wanting something more, complaining about their sad lot in life.

Observation four: *Being married makes life more complicated, but faith in Christ can enhance, not diminish, both the quality of marriage and of your life.*

In 1 Corinthians 7 the Apostle Paul actually builds an argument for singleness. You and I need to be careful not to put down singleness. Paul was not anti-marriage. He is writing about having an undivided devotion to the Lord. He notes that when two people get married their lives become much more complicated. He states it bluntly, '... But those who marry will face many troubles in this life...' (1 Cor. 7:28).

How true that is! It is not easy to be married today in the culture in which we live. And it wasn't easy to be married in the first century. Marriage has never been easy. There are enormous pressures on marriage. We are kidding ourselves if we pretend otherwise.

You and I who are married are observing a horrendous satanic attack on marriage and the home. Few of us are exempt from it. Divorce is increasing at an exponential rate to the point that it panics our children. Think of how many of them and their friends come from divorced homes. Some of us born before 1945 never even considered the possibility that our parents would get a divorce. It simply wasn't a viable possibility. Today, a serious disagreement between a husband and wife, some intense stress that leads to increasingly frequent arguments, or simply the pattern of casual, on-going bickering into which some of us can stumble, can signal to our children that the next painful reality will be divorce. The very idea that two people can fall in love and then fall out of love only serves to exacerbate these fears.

Our relationship to Jesus can give stability to a marriage. God's Word furnishes the ideals and guidelines for meaningful commitment. Our own personal relationship with Jesus Christ, in which he forgives us and stands by us, models what it is to forgive and stand by our partner. It presents us with a basis for analyzing and rejecting the many inadequate models for relationships that are promoted in secular society today.

We need to look our children directly in the eyes and say, 'Yes, we have our differences, but we are committed to each other in Christ – even when we get on each other's nerves, are insensitive to each other, or have other serious differences that we are struggling to resolve. With God's help, we are prepared to work out our difficulties and forgive each other and even get some outside help if that is necessary.'

Don't minimize the importance of renewed commitment of your vows to God, to your partner, and to your children – in an honest acknowledgment that every marriage has problems and even the healthiest of marriages will have times of trouble. You will have to figure out for yourselves the best way to renew your vows. This may involve a simple, quiet, internal, prayerful recommitment, talking this through with the Lord in prayer. You may then want to write a note or send a card, expressing in writing to your partner the essence of this renewed commitment. I have noticed in recent years many couples wanting formal ceremonies of 'renewed vows'. This works for many. Anne and I have not officially done this, nor do I encourage couples into such formal renewals, in that I see this as much more of an ongoing, continuing process than a dramatic two-step, marriage followed by renewal of vows 25 or 30 years later. However, this may be the perfect statement you need to make to reassure each other of the seriousness of your commitment. Remember, there is a major distinction between being 'in love' and choosing 'to love'.

C. S. Lewis describes the absurdity of maintaining the feeling of 'being in love' that two persons have the day before they are married and throughout the next fifty years. In fact, it would be highly undesirable if it could be. He writes:

> Who could bear to live in that excitement for even five years? What would become of your work, your appetite, your sleep, your friendships? But, of course, ceasing to be 'in love' need not mean ceasing to love. Love in this second sense – love as distinct from 'being in love' – is not merely a feeling. It is a deep unity, maintained by the will and deliberately strengthened by habit; reinforced by (in Christian marriages) the grace which both partners ask, and receive, from God. They can have this love for each other even at those moments when they do not like each other; as you love yourself even when you do not like yourself. They can retain this love even when each would easily, if they allowed themselves, be 'in love' with someone else. 'Being in love' first moved them to promise fidelity; this quieter love enables them to keep the promise.

Observation five: *Watch out for that destructive word 'incompatibility'.*

The difference between a healthy and unhealthy marriage is that in a healthy marriage the couple acknowledges that they have problems, knowing that, with Christ's help, nothing is too big to handle. Apparent incompatibility doesn't have to doom a marriage to failure.

Problems don't have to break up your marriage. In fact, problems can be the stabilizing, cohesive factor, which can cement your marriage together with greater firmness.

Jesus declared, 'In this world you will have trouble'. He voiced this sophisticated understanding of the nature of humankind both within society at large and within the husband-wife relationship. He warned his followers that this world is not an easy place in which to live. He was quick to bring into focus a realistic look at human nature, outlining the implications for us today caused by the sinful rebellion of Adam and Eve.

Fascinating, isn't it, to discover that Jesus did not couple a pessimistic spirit with his realistic understanding of life. Instead, he called his followers to hope, saying, 'But take courage. I have overcome the world'. In this spirit, he talked about marriage, pointing out the sanctity of the husband-wife relationship, quoting the Old Testament book of Genesis. When questioned about the permissibility of divorce, Jesus answered:

> 'Haven't you read,' he replied, 'that at the beginning the Creator "made them male and female", and said, "For this reason a man will leave his father and mother and be united to his wife, and the two will become one flesh"? So they are no longer two, but one. Therefore what God has joined together, let man not separate' (Matt. 19:4-6).

Jesus articulated the sanctity of marriage. He was quick to understand the sinful nature of all men and women, which could ultimately corrupt the husband-wife relationship. He acknowledged that this sin could so affect the man-woman relationship that, in extreme circumstances, the two could not continue to live together. Yet he viewed divorce as an absolute last resort. It is permissible only in the most extreme cases of infidelity, desertion, and abuse of the relationship, where cruelty threatens to destroy the other person.

In contemporary words, Jesus was warning against the use of the term 'incompatibility'.

Watch out for that word. It is one of the most destructive, suggestive words in the English language. Certainly your marriage has its problems. There is something wrong with you or your partner if either of you is perfect. You are a freak if you are perfect. Your relationship is abnormal if it is free of difficulty.

The present marriage statistics point out that too many couples, when confronted with the normal, routine problems of marriage, throw up their hands and say, 'Well, I guess we are *incompatible!*' as they make their way to the divorce court.

The Swiss psychiatrist Paul Tournier suggests that we exorcize this term 'incompatibility' from our vocabulary. When I first read what he wrote I wanted to argue with him because I had seen couples who I had thought were incompatible. But the longer I have mused on this, counseled couples, and observed my own relationship with Anne, the more convinced I am of the truth of what he stated in his book, *To Understand Each Other*:

> So-called emotional incompatibility is a myth invented by jurists short of arguments in order to plead for divorce. It is likewise a common excuse people use in order to hide their own feelings. I simply do not believe it exists. There are no emotional incompatibilities. There are misunderstandings and mistakes, however, which can be corrected where there is the willingness to do so.

Tournier is basically saying that incompatibility is a word that we have created to give us an excuse to quit working at a relationship.

I know one couple who are total opposites. You would never think they could make a marriage work. He's an introverted scholar who lives his life in the world of ideas and in the solitude of a corner carrel in the library. He does everything he can to avoid contact with people except to emerge when necessary to teach, attend official social obligations, and do what is necessary in terms of family interaction. She is the ultimate extrovert. People energize her. The more social action, the more she thrives. Obviously, they found in each other that disowned part of themselves. But can this marriage work? It has. Each of them has had to work hard to try to understand how the other is wired. And, at times, it has taken some individual, couple, and family therapy. The children needed help to understand some of the confusing family dynamics. These two could have backed away from each other, concluding early in their marriage that they were simply incompatible. Instead, they refused to entertain that notion. They have not only worked at their relationship, they have also celebrated their differences, finding ways to maximize a synergy in marriage in which the two of them together, with all of their differences, are much greater than they could possibly be going their separate directions. Every time I see them, I thank God for the example they give to me and others that the greatest temperamental differences can be transformed into a marvelously effective marriage when two people are willing to recognize their needs and seek the help of God and good therapists.

Let's face it. Adjustments are necessary. We need to make all kinds of adjustments in order to handle life's problems. Let's look at three basic forms of *adjustments*.

One type is the adjustment of *compromise*. Husbands and wives need to compromise constantly, which means finding a middle ground that's satisfactory to both so neither has to make too great a sacrifice.

The second type of adjustment is *accommodation*. When two people have seriously opposing viewpoints or antagonistic characteristics, instead of fighting their way through life, they learn to accommodate each other. They may not be able to find a compromise that is entirely satisfactory, so they accommodate each other – with no expressed aggression or antagonism. They develop an equilibrium. They both may realize that they have not reached a satisfactory agreement, but their accommodation removes most of the strain upon the marriage.

A third form of adjustment is *hostility*. Constant quarreling and bickering begin at the points where the husband and wife differ. Or lingering tension is produced by anger that is sometimes expressed in words and often made evident by their behavior. Unable to cope with their differences, they reach an *impasse* – a static, inflexible hardening of the relationship that is marked by hostility.

Let me try to illustrate these three approaches to adjusting by a hypothetical couple. She loves to ski. He enjoys sailing. For them to compromise might mean that they would divide their vacation time and the finances available to do together what each enjoys the most. For them to accommodate each other might be for them to take separate vacations without resent-ment and snide remarks – graciously accepting that one gets seasick and the other is scared of high places, or they just don't enjoy each other's favorite sports. The adjustment of hostility is not difficult to imagine. The resentments build up as they battle over their vacations, creating an environment of warfare on this somewhat trivial matter and on many more important areas of disagreement.

A healthy marriage has its problems. However, the two peo-ple refuse to let them solidify. They work toward the healthy adjustments – compromise and accommodation – bending over backwards to understand each other's feelings. They cultivate their love, which can still be present, even when there are seem-ingly irreconcilable differences of attitude and temperament. This couple has a realistic understanding – that marriage is a relationship between two adults. It's not for children. If your fourteen-year-old daughter came to you with stars in her eyes and said, 'Mommy, I've found the perfect guy. I want to get married!' – what would you do? In one way or another, you would get the fact across that she's still a child. She's not ready for marriage. Unfortunately, some of us, who by chronology are adults, are emotionally still teenagers. If we are going to have vital marriages, we must approach them as adults, realizing that maturity is the capacity to postpone immediate gratification for the ultimate good. We can develop a love relationship by looking to the well-being of our partner instead of our own personal happiness.

The Apostle Paul strips away all of our sentimental, phony definitions as he writes:

> This love of which I speak is slow to lose patience – it looks for a way of being constructive. It is not possessive: it is neither anxious to impress nor does it cherish inflated ideas of its own importance.
>
> Love has good manners and does not pursue selfish advantage. It is not touchy. It does not keep account of evil or gloat over the wickedness of other people. On the contrary, it is glad with all good men when truth prevails.
>
> Love knows no limit to its endurance, no end to its trust, no fading of its hope; it can outlast anything. It is, in fact, the one thing that still stands when all else has fallen (1 Cor. 13:4-8, Phillips).

This is the antidote to incompatibility. It helps you adjust yourself to your partner. It strips away self-pity, grudge-holding, and the petty criticisms that destroy the husband-wife relationship. This is a Christian understanding of the husband-wife relationship. It bases itself on the New Testament of love that is so different from the contemporary ideal. It is easy to mistake sexual attraction for love. It is easy to give yourself to someone who deserves your love. How much more difficult it is to give yourself to someone who is resistant to you? This is the love Christ showed for His Church and the love a husband and wife are privileged to show to each other. This is *unconditional love*. This is love that does not strike a bargain. This love does not say, 'I will scratch your back if you scratch mine.'

If you are willing to love this way, you are set free from the incompatibilities that can destroy your marriage. This means that you are faithful to your partner, even when he or she does not live up to his or her responsibilities. You are faithful whether your partner is a believer or nonbeliever in Jesus Christ. If you resist, you are resisting God who has instructed you to adapt. Your marriage will take on a whole new quality if you realize that the buck stops with you.

There are four words I would like to leave with you, words which I'm trying to remember in my relationship with Anne.

Word one: *Triangle*
You and I have to face the fact that a healthy marriage is a triangle affair. It involves a husband and wife and a third party. That party is Jesus Christ. As you and I are able to bow our knees to him, allowing him to be part of our relationship, we are much more able to find a healthy oneness with our marriage partner. You need to open your life to Jesus Christ, admitting to him that you are a sinner. Let him know the mistakes you've made in your marriage. Don't worry, he already knows them. But if you just restate them, you will find a release. Ask him to forgive you and then daily spend some time with him alone. The worst days of my marriage are those days when I have not spent any time alone with God. Let your Bible become an open book. Ask the Holy Spirit to convict you of sin, pointing out where you are wrong. Ask the Lord for his help, his strength. He wants you to succeed. He wants your marriage to be a happy experience. Let the symmetry of the two of you kneeling at the altar in humble worship of the God of the universe whose name is Jesus Christ be the defining symbol of your marriage.

Word two: *Commitment*
Remember that marriage is meant to be permanent. Remind yourself periodically of your marriage vows, which go something like this: 'I take you to be my wedded partner and I do promise and covenant before God and these witnesses to be your loving and faithful partner, in plenty and in want, in joy

and in sorrow, in sickness and in health, as long as we both shall live.'

Is there any greater, all-encompassing promise a person could make? If you take your marriage vows seriously, you are saying that no matter what you do to me or no matter what life throws at us, I will be faithful to you until the day one of us dies. That covers the ups and downs of marital life. It handles the emotional upsets. It guards the two of you in the days of physical sickness. It protects you against being discarded by your partner when he discovers someone a bit prettier or more interesting. It protects your partner against being discarded by you when she's not at her best. Many a man will cheat at marriage who wouldn't consider breaking his word in business. A contract is a contract. Your honor is pretty important. Frankly, it's worth keeping the covenant even when you don't feel like it. And there are times when the best of people don't feel like it.

Word three: *Communication*
Nothing puts a couple more at ease than to know that they are communicating. Even differences of opinion can be joyously expressed when there is an honest, non-hostile grappling with diversity. Some of the greatest times in our marriage are when Anne and I, discovering that we have allowed daily events to push us apart, sit down and talk. We air our differences. We ask the Lord to forgive us. We wrestle creatively with how we can improve our marriage. We plan together. We laugh together. We cry together. We pray together. That's communication. At times it gets painful. Painful because it involves honesty. Honesty is basic to communication.

Word four: *Humor*
A sense of humor is essential to a creative marriage. When I say humor, I mean the capacity to laugh at yourself, not at your partner. I find this quality indispensable to all my activities of life. If I have one besetting sin it is of taking myself too seriously. This is, in effect, another way of spelling *pride*!

If you can laugh at yourself, you may be able to tolerate a chuckle or two from your partner, as together, with the Lord's help, you develop a relationship for the future.

I would be the last to pretend that marriage is easy. But I would be the first to challenge you to take a realistic look at marriage in all of its complexities. Find the forgiveness of the Lord and his fresh beginning and the mutual forgiveness between you and your partner. If necessary, get the help of a gifted professional to work through the issues and complexities of your relationship, making it into what will never be a perfect marriage but can be a much healthier marriage. And if your partner won't get help, seek help yourself to work through your issues in a way that at least you have made some personal growth and contributed to the potential healing of the relationship.

Almost four decades of marriage has convinced me of two basic facts of life.

Fact of life one: Neither you nor I can have a perfect marriage.
Fact of life two: Neither you nor I would really want one.

The whole idea is sort of crazy that two people can fall in love and live happily ever after. How boring! The fact is that we are human. We are different. We are all sinners, having fallen short of what God dreams for us to be. The glorious reality is that God redeems us by his grace and energizes us by his Holy Spirit to live creatively together, acknowledging our imperfections and rejoicing in our gifts. We have the privilege of changing what we can change in ourselves in order to make a more positive contribution to family living. And we also have the sacred opportunity to accept our spouse and children the way they are, giving them the same gift of understanding that they will hopefully share with us. No, you can't have a perfect marriage – and you wouldn't want one. There are no perfect marriages. But you can have a healthy marriage!

# CHAPTER 11
## SEX AND MARRIAGE

*Flee from sexual immorality. All other sins a man commits are outside his body, but he who sins sexually sins against his own body. Do you not know that your body is a temple of the Holy Spirit, who is in you, whom you have received from God? You are not your own; you were bought at a price. Therefore honor God with your body*

1 Corinthians 6:18-20

Can you think of any topic that comes up more frequently than sex?

You and I can't read a newspaper, open a magazine, turn on TV, go to a movie, or tune in to a talk show without being barraged with sex.

Even common, ordinary conversation is increasingly laced through with sexual innuendo. So many of our jokes, personal stories, asides, make oblique or even frontal reference to sex.

And then there are our private thoughts. Who of us is exempt from a fascination with the topic?

I dare you to turn on the television and make it through a night of TV without finding someone climbing into bed with someone to whom he or she is not married. I dare you to make it through a day at the office without hearing an off-colored joke. I dare you to pick up the newspaper without finding some scandal or sexually explicit advertisement.

Yet, no topic gets addressed less frequently in any kind of sustained practical, biblical, theological conversation. I, as a pastor, have learned that this is such an emotionally charged topic that I'm better to leave it alone. Granted, I'm forced to address it when I do systematic, biblical exposition through an entire book of the Bible. The Bible has a lot to say about sex. So I can't avoid talking about it on those occasions when the next few verses address the topic of adultery, fornication, sexual immorality, and how God, who created us as sexual persons, dreams for us to use our sexuality in healthy ways.

Our failure to address this topic in a healthy, systematic way has produced unfortunate results. Recently, the chaplains at the University of Nebraska took a survey of incoming freshmen and asked them the question, 'How much influence did your church play in your views of sexuality?' Of the freshmen who were surveyed, two percent said that their church had anything to do with their views of sexuality. Some of the comments that they also included in the survey are worth quoting:

'People in my church don't believe in sex.'

'Our church is boring. They don't talk about sex or dating or marriage. It's probably just as well; they'd make that boring as well.'

'In our youth group, we talked about sex some but avoided the juicy stuff.'

If it's true that the church doesn't talk about sex, then we're the only ones.

The newest studies say 21 percent of men and 15 percent of women have had intercourse by the time they were 14 years old. In some parts of the country, 82 percent of the people have had intercourse by the time they were 19. Those in the upper income brackets have had more premarital sex and extramarital sex than those in lower income brackets. Thirty percent of those who indicated that they were religious said they also had extramarital affairs. And 70 percent of those who said they were religious acknowledged having had premarital sex.

So, we're talking not about *them* but about *us*! That's why we need more serious, biblical, theological talk about sexuality.

In a most positive way, the Bible declares the importance of human sexuality when in Genesis 2:18-25 we read:

'The Lord God said, "It is not good for the man to be alone. I will make a helper suitable for him."

'Now the Lord God had formed out of the ground all the beasts of the field and all the birds of the air. He brought them to the man to see what he would name them; and whatever the man called each living creature, that was its name. So the man gave names to all the livestock, the birds of the air and all the beasts of the field.

'But for Adam no suitable helper was found. So the Lord God caused the man to fall into a deep sleep; and while he was sleeping, he took one of the man's ribs and closed up the place with flesh. Then the Lord God made a woman from the rib he had taken out of the man, and he brought her to the man.

'The man said,
"This is now bone of my bones
and flesh of my flesh;
she shall be called 'woman',
for she was taken out of man."

'For this reason a man will leave his father and mother and be united to his wife, and they will become one flesh.

'The man and his wife were both naked, and they felt no shame' (Gen. 2:18-25).


From the very beginning we have been created with a desire to have a partner. It is the very part of God's design. And with this comes the reality and the thrilling potential of human sexuality.

Craig Barnes, the pastor of the National Presbyterian Church in Washington, D.C., has stated: 'Now it's important for Christians occasionally to remind themselves that God did not create you as a soul and then just wrap a disposable body around it that isn't important. Rather, according to the text, he created you as a body and *then* he brought that body to life by giving you a soul. That means that the body and the soul are intricately related. What your body yearns for is symptomatic of the yearning of your soul.'

All through human history there has been this struggle be-tween the positive, creative uses of human sexuality and those pornographic distortions of it. It's no accident that prostitution is referred to as 'the world's oldest profession'. It makes sense that from ancient times to the present, men and women have created gods and goddesses of fertility. We have our own in-ternal battle between the negative and positive uses of human sexuality. This doesn't come out of the blue. It's part of the very definition of what it is to be human: people created in the image of God, people who have rebelled against God, people who are in need of the grace of our Lord Jesus Christ.

C. S. Lewis has done a superb job of describing our con-temporary struggles with human sexuality. In his post World War II broadcast essays for the British Broadcasting Company, which were later compiled into that classic book titled *Mere Christianity*, he wrote:

> The Christian idea of marriage is based on Christ's words that a man and wife are to be regarded as a single organism – for that is what the words 'one flesh' would be in modern English. And the Christians believe that when he said this he was not expressing a sentiment but stating a fact – just as one is stating a fact when one says that a lock and its key are one mechanism, or that a violin and a bow are one musical instrument. The inventor of a human machine was telling us that its two halves, the male and the female, were made to be combined together in pairs, not simply on the sexual level, but totally combined. The monstrosity of sexual intercourse outside marriage is that those who indulge in it are trying to isolate one kind of union (the sexual) from all the other kinds of union which were intended to go along with it and make up the total union. The Christian attitude does not mean that there is anything wrong about sexual pleasure, any more than about the pleasure of eating. It means that you must not isolate that pleasure and try to get the pleasures of taste without swallowing and digesting, by chewing things and spitting them out again....

Christianity is almost the only one of the great religions which thoroughly approves of the body – which believes that matter is good, that God himself once took on a human body, that some kind of body is going to be given to us even in Heaven and is going to be an essential part of our happiness, our beauty, and our energy. Christianity has glorified marriage more than any other religion: and nearly all the greatest love poetry in the world has been produced by Christians. If anyone says that sex, in itself, is bad, Christianity contradicts him at once....

Chastity is the most unpopular of the Christian virtues. There is no getting away from it: the old Christian rule is, 'Either marriage, with complete faithfulness to your partner, or else total abstinence'. Now this is so difficult and so contrary to our instincts, that obviously either Christianity is wrong or our sexual instinct, as it now is, has gone wrong. One or the other. Of course, being a Christian, I think it is the instinct which has gone wrong.... You can get a large audience together for a strip-tease act – that is to watch a girl undress on the stage. Now suppose you came to a country where you could fill a theatre by simply bringing a covered plate on to the stage and then slowly lifting the cover so as to let every one see, just before the lights went out, that it contained a mutton chop or a bit of bacon, would you not think that in that country something had gone wrong with the appetite for food? And would not anyone who had grown up in a different world think there was something equally queer about the state of the sex instinct among us?

During my four decades as a pastor, I have heard both in the private setting of my counseling study and in public settings some tough but important questions about sex.

Question: *Just what does God have to say about premarital or extra-marital sex?*

The answer is that God forbids adultery. Adultery is defined as a married man or woman having sexual intercourse with a person to whom they are not married. The Bible also forbids fornication. The Bible defines fornication as every kind of sexual intercourse outside of marriage.

Let me share just a few of the biblical statements in which God speaks about adultery and fornication.

Exodus 20:14 reads: 'You shall not commit adultery.'

Proverbs 5:3-6 reads:

> For the lips of an adulteress drip honey,
>   and her speech is smoother than oil;
> but in the end she is bitter as gall,
>   sharp as a double-edged sword.
> Her feet go down to death;
>   her steps lead straight to the grave.
> She gives no thought to the way of life;
>   her paths are crooked, but she knows it not.

Proverbs 6:23-32 reads:

> For these commands are a lamp,
>   this teaching is a light,
> and the corrections of discipline
>   are the way to life,
> keeping you from the immoral woman,
>   from the smooth tongue of the wayward wife.
> Do not lust in your heart after her beauty
>   or let her captivate you with her eyes,
> for the prostitute reduces you to a loaf of bread,
>   and the adulteress preys upon your very life.
> Can a man scoop fire into his lap
>   without his clothes being burned?
> Can a man walk on hot coals
>   without his feet being scorched?
> So is he who sleeps with another man's wife;
>   no one who touches her will go unpunished.
> Men do not despise a thief if he steals
>   to satisfy his hunger when he is starving.

Yet if he is caught, he must pay sevenfold,
    though it costs him all the wealth of his house.
But a man who commits adultery lacks judgment;
    whoever does so destroys himself.

Jesus said succinctly in the Sermon on the Mount, recorded in Matthew 5:27-28:

'You have heard that it was said, "Do not commit adultery". But I tell you that anyone who looks at a woman lustfully has already committed adultery with her in his heart.'

Galatians 5:19-21 reads:

The acts of the sinful nature are obvious: sexual immorality, impurity and debauchery; idolatry and witchcraft; hatred, discord, jealousy, fits of rage, selfish ambition, dissensions, factions and envy; drunkenness, orgies, and the like. I warn you, as I did before, that those who live like this will not inherit the kingdom of God.

And Paul writes to the Corinthians in 1 Corinthians 6:13-20:

The body is not meant for sexual immorality, but for the Lord, and the Lord for the body. By his power God raised the Lord from the dead, and he will raise us also. Do you not know that your bodies are members of Christ himself? Shall I then take the members of Christ and unite them with a prostitute? Never! Do you not know that he who unites himself with a prostitute is one with her in body? For it is said, 'The two will become one flesh'. But he who unites himself with the Lord is one with him in spirit. Flee from sexual immorality. All other sins a man commits are outside his body, but he who sins sexually sins against his own body. Do you not know that your body is a temple of the Holy Spirit, who is in you, whom you have received from God? You are not your own; you were bought at a price. Therefore honor God with your body.

God has this and much more to say about sex.

Question: *Why has God taken such a strong position on premarital and extramarital sex?*

Is God some antiquated, arthritic, great-grandfather in the sky who gives us all these inflaming hormones and then says 'no' – because he doesn't want us to have all the fun when he can't? Some see him as this.

No! God wants you and me to live the smart way!

Sexual sin, by its very definition and reality, is de-humanizing. You and I become merely animals when we divorce our sexual drives from the fact that we as human beings are created in the very image of God.

A person's determination to believe they're smarter than God when it comes to the use of sexuality will ultimately backfire. It destroys you. And it destroys others. That's why God is so strict. No, he's not some sex-starved, angry old grandfather trying to destroy our fun. Not for a moment! He created sex. He wants it to be channeled for your and my very best interests. Far from his commands being negativistic and inhibiting, they are guides to the healthiest kind of sexual living possible. Analyze contemporary life and see how sensible are his commands. In fact, even if one is not a believer in Jesus Christ and has no respect for biblical teaching, there are some good, common-sense reasons for avoiding premarital or extramarital intercourse.

One is the possibility of *unwanted pregnancy*.

Yes, even with the pill, the frequency of unwanted pregnancies continues to increase. The incidence of unwed mothers has reached endemic proportions. What is more tragic than for a child to be brought into this world unwanted? I have spent hours at a time with women impregnated out of wedlock. I've watched young couples, who once thought they were in love, struggle with the decision of whether to marry. Abortion is one way out. But it has serious moral and psychological considerations when it is used to simply cover up a mistake. It is not a valid method of contraception! There is no foolproof method of contraception. Many young people are not well enough informed. Sometimes romantic ideas prevent necessary precautions. Sometimes contraceptives are difficult for the young person to obtain. And condoms have proven not to be failsafe. The couple who thinks they are safe all too often become pregnant. Although the pill is considered by most doctors to be foolproof, those taking it are not. Either by simple forgetfulness, momentary romanticism, or some deep-seated inner motivation to conceive in order to hold that fellow can cause a pregnancy that surprises one if not both.

Two is the danger of *sexual disease.*

Venereal disease has not been checked by modern medicine. The increased incidence of sexual promiscuity has brought about a tragic, soaring incidence of diseases. Never does a week go by that our major newspapers and magazines haven't featured stories on AIDS. You and I can't even begin to keep up on the statistical forward march of this killer, sexually transmitted disease. Each year, here in the United States, more people are killed by AIDS than U.S. soldiers during the entire course of the Vietnam War. Since the beginning of the HIV/AIDS epidemic through the beginning of the year 2000 an estimated 450,000 have died in North America and 16.3 million world wide, 2.6 million of these deaths were in the year 1999. And an additional 920,000 in North America and 33.6 million world wide are living with HIV/AIDS. These statistics were released by the United Nations.

Thus far, we're talking only about AIDS. Now most schools are offering classes on sexually transmitted diseases. Genital herpes, syphilis, hepatitis, and pelvic inflammatory disease are added to the specter of AIDS. The last statistic I saw came from the Director of the Sexually Transmitted Disease Division of the Federal Center for Disease Control who stated that about 13 million people each year, here in the United States, contract a sexually transmitted disease. These illnesses cost the country billions of dollars and create untold human misery.

If you want to read a tragic story of what venereal disease can do to a person, read William Manchester's biography of Winston Churchill in which he describes how Churchill's father, Lord Randolph Churchill, contracted syphilis through promiscuous sexual involvement. He describes how this promising, British politician gradually eroded in the very public eye and over a period of years self-destructed and died. You read a few stories like that from secular biographies, and they make you think that God's ways, far from being negative, are positive.

Let me share with you a counseling issue I am increasingly facing. A married person comes in and tells me that they've discovered their partner has been unfaithful. They are literally scared to death. Although they are prepared to accept their partner's repentance and to offer forgiveness, they fear that they might become the inadvertent victim of a venereal disease. They fear where their partner may have been and picked it up. A number have told me how they painfully have had to tell their spouse, 'No sex until you have been tested for AIDS'. Think that through. That has a profound impact on a relationship, doesn't it?

Three is that many men are bent on *conquest to prove their masculinity.*

I pity the woman who gets trapped into this false situation. If only she could listen in for a few minutes to the conversation in the men's locker room she would take much less seriously the romantic pleadings, 'If you really love me, you wouldn't say no!' And now, with women's liberation, the stereotypical view of men being more interested in sex than women is no longer the case. How often we read about women who – having no desire for a love relationship and marriage – are simply on the market looking for the ideal male by whom they become pregnant.

Four is that *premarital and extramarital sex can be personally destruc-tive, emotionally, psychologically, and spiritually.*

It's habit-forming. In most cases it's not something that a couple does once or twice and quits doing. It develops a personal dependence wherein no real ultimate commitment has been agreed upon. It is an agonizing experience for a pastor to deal with the emotional, physical, and spiritual fragmentation that often is the experience of the man or the woman who has just been jilted. Sex is a much more serious matter than some of us would like to admit. It is symbolic of commitment, even when that commitment is not really there. If you are ready for sex, you are ready for marriage! Watch out for excuses that really don't stand the light of day.

I talk with an increasing number of couples who have post-poned marriage – but have starting living together – because they say they don't have enough money saved up for the kind of wedding they would like. Who are they trying to impress? How much better to have a modest wedding, if you're now ready to get married, than to move in with each other without that ultimate commitment.

Five is that premarital or extramarital sex is *not a reliable test of sexual compatibility.*

Many a man has told me, 'I would never marry a woman without trying her out first.' He might just be surprised to find that there is a major difference between sex outside and inside marriage. Secrecy surrounding premarital sex often heightens one's excitement. Needless to say, both will be on their very best behavior, knowing that their failure to perform could lead to the end of the relationship. How different is sex in marriage where both have the security of ultimate commitment. Sex is not geared to one's having to meet a particular standard. It is meant to share in the most intimate way possible a way that will procreate and also bring personal fulfillment. A normal, healthy man and a normal, healthy woman, both from a physiological and an emotional standpoint, should be able to find sexual compatibility. In those cases where there is some question about the possibility of compatibility and sexual function, premarital experimentation will not necessarily give the correct answer.

Six is that *an obsessive interest in sex is often created.*

I have talked with couples who have slipped into a *sexual* relationship before marriage who find that sex is all they think about. Whereas they used to have fun dating and being with other people, their life is pretty much geared toward sex. This is no way to live. A happily married couple spends a very small fraction of their time having sex compared to all the other activities that fill their lives. Obsessive interest in sex is abnormal.

Seven is that premarital sex can *have a marring, spoiling effect on a later marriage.*

What I mean by that is that it can breed a later misunderstanding between two people who were weak before marriage, giving into their impulses. There is always uncertainty. You know that your partner could, once again, be weak and move into an extramarital affair. There is always a potential of resentment going into marriage. I have talked with individuals who idealize waiting until marriage, but one pressured the other into premarital sex. Granted, they had agreed to it, but they carry with them conflicted feelings that can color their future relationship. This is why, in my premarital counseling, I urge couples to honestly face up to the relationship they have, laying aside any rationalizations that they manufacture. They can honestly discuss their disobedience to God and claim his forgiveness. They can go into their marriage with a much greater sense of integrity and honesty than otherwise would be present.

There are many other common-sense reasons for avoiding premarital and extramarital intercourse. Simply stated, it is impossible to achieve in a premarital or extramarital relationship a spiritual, emotional, psychological, and mental bonding – a oneness of the ultimate commitment that is possible in

Christian marriage. The potential for heartbreak and shattered dreams is enormous. To put it bluntly, it is smart to wait until marriage. And it's smart to remain faithful inside of marriage. God's way is not designed to spoil your fun. God's way is the smart, the intelligent way.

Question: *Just how important is sex to a healthy marriage?*
It is very important. It isn't everything, but it does provide the potential for enhanced relational joy and multi-dimensional emotional, spiritual, as well as physical, bonding.

Question: *How much sex is realistic in marriage?*
As much as you both can agree you want. We each have our own needs and desires. For some they are greater than for others. Those needs and the desired frequency of sex can fluctuate throughout a marriage. A couple with healthful communication can be honest with each other about their true feelings. Compromises will need to be reached. One may need to agree to greater frequency, while the other may need to somewhat modify his or her expectations. Sometimes a pastor or therapist can function as a helpful third party to facilitate understanding and communication leading to greater mutual sexual fulfillment. Let's not forget that the Hollywood image of bedroom sexual heroics is much more fantasy than a reality. We need to be realistic in both our expectations and our capabilities to perform. Loving communication is the key. There will be times when stress or illness may inhibit or prohibit overt sexual behavior for a while. But nothing need stop snuggling, tenderness, intimate conversation and mutually expressed care.

Question: *How does one talk with your kids about sex?*
The same way you talk about anything else that is important. That's right. We often make too big a deal about this and then are afraid to even bring up the topic. Don't push it on your kids with overkill. I tried that, and it backfired. They will let you know how deep to go with the topic. Just make it clear from

their earliest age that it is not a taboo topic. It is a healthy part of life. Let them know that sex is good as it is used wisely. And make it clear that there is no question that is out of bounds, that you will be honest with them and, as much as you are going to communicate a biblical view of sex, you'll try not to preach.

Question: *What's all this talk about sexual addiction?*
It is possible in a society as conflicted about our sexuality as we have today for well-meaning persons to drift into patterns of premarital and extramarital sexual behavior that are addicting. Those lifestyles are often not altered by marriage.

I have a pastor friend who for several decades maintained a strong public ministry while behind the scenes rationalizing extramarital flirtations, lunches, physical intimacies – some stopping just short of intercourse and some involving inter-course. On several occasions he came close to getting help, but his rationalizations accentuated his denial. Finally, three of his closest friends participated in an intervention that led to his seeking help. Finally, he was forced to resign his church. He now says it took that to bring him out of his denial and to really begin doing the in-depth work necessary to confront both his addiction and to deal healthfully with his marriage.

I'll never forget the conversation I had with him two months after the President Clinton–Monica Lewinsky allegations first surfaced. My pastor friend, now restored to ministry after four years of suspension plus continuing therapy, declared, 'Clinton is as guilty as heck!' I asked, 'How can you be so sure? Give the man a break! I'm willing to believe his denials. Isn't a man innocent until proven guilty?' His response was, 'I know he's guilty because he's using all of my favorite lines. I recognize his rationalizations. He's living in denial!' Months later, the emerging truth proved him correct.

Good help is available to those willing to confront their sexual addictions.

Question: *But what about our kids? I hold to this biblical, sexual ethic but my kids don't. What do I do, write them off?*

Absolutely not! They're still your children. They are traumatized by the epidemic of divorce. They're scared to death to make a commitment. They think they're beating the system. This is no excuse for their behavior. It's disobedience to God. And it's not the smart way to live!

You don't have to buy into a wrong lifestyle to love your children. You can be honest and lovingly say why you believe this is wrong. At the same time, you can still love them, respect them for their giftedness, and pray that God will bring them to their senses before it is too late. We dare not fail to love. And we dare not declare what the Bible calls sin to no longer be sin!

Question: *But what about me? I'm involved in premarital or extramarital sex. How does God view me? What can I do about this?*

God views you the same way you, as a loving parent, hopefully view a child of yours who messes up his life. God views you with love. God views you with compassion. God views you with a heart that wants to forgive where there's genuine repentance. God views you with a desire to help you live a healthful existence.

Question: *Isn't sex sin the unforgivable sin?*
No way!

A sex sin is serious. It breaks down relationship with God and relationship with other persons. It has its serious, lasting consequences. But there's only one unforgivable sin. That's the 'blasphemy of the Holy Spirit'. That's when you and I refuse to admit that we're sinners and accept God's all-sufficient grace, his unmerited favor.

The Apostle Paul makes a wonderful statement of hope to those of us who are willing to admit our sinful behavior and our sinful attitudes. He makes this very serious observation in 1 Corinthians 6:9-10: 'Do you not know that the wicked will not inherit the kingdom of God? Do not be deceived: Neither the sexually immoral nor idolaters nor adulterers nor male prostitutes nor homosexual offenders nor thieves nor the greedy nor drunkards nor slanderers nor swindlers will inherit the kingdom of God.' Then he adds this liberating observation in the immediately following verse, 1 Corinthians 9:11: 'And that is what some of you were. But you were washed, you were sanctified, you were justified in the name of the Lord Jesus Christ and by the Spirit of our God.'

The first-century church was filled with men and women whose lives had been messed up by sin, just as is the church at the beginning of the twenty-first century. They, like we, lived in a culture that at times was a moral cesspool. The Good News of the Gospel is that Jesus Christ meets you and me where we are, lifting us out, cleaning us up, to present us faultless before the Father based on his atoning work on the cross.

The expectation is repentance on our part. We need to admit it when we're wrong. Jesus forgave the woman caught in the very act of adultery. He challenged her to go and sin no more. At the same time, he pointed the finger of judgment at those self-righteous men who had castigated her for her sin by challenging the one in their number without sin to cast the first stone. Those fellows disappeared very fast.

God wants you and me to realize that sexual experience has a way of running down when two persons are united at the pelvis only. That produces a restlessness of spirit that is precisely the opposite God had in mind when he designed us as sexual persons.

So-called new sexual freedom has, in an ironic way, both trivialized sex and also made it oppressive. It has taken the sacred out of sex, reducing it to the familiarity of a handshake.

If you're living together, without the benefit of a lifelong commitment in marriage, I suggest you confront the reality, ask God's forgiveness, move out, and remain celibate until you're married. I know a number of couples that have taken that drastic action and in the process have found a respect for themselves as individuals and respect for each other as a couple. They've experienced God's grace and have learned that quality of maturity that is the capacity to postpone immediate gratification for the ultimate good.

Move up the wedding date if necessary. But for God's sake and yours, bring your life into conformity with the way God designed it to function.

If adultery has been your lifestyle, come to the Lord. Ask for his forgiveness. Get the pastoral and psychological help available to move beyond that which is destructive into the wholeness of what God dreams for you and your spouse. And be a participant in that amazing grace of our Lord Jesus Christ who offers forgiveness and the strength to live one day at a time as he, by his Holy Spirit, enables you to experience in all its fullness the sexuality with which he designed you to function.

# CHAPTER 12
## MYTHS THAT CAN DESTROY A MARRIAGE

*Have nothing to do with godless myths and old wives' tales; rather train yourself to be godly*

1 Timothy 4:7

It started out one kind of evening and ended up another.

Anne and I were out for dinner. It was a pleasant evening with a couple who come to St. Andrew's and another couple who were hosting the four of us in their home.

The hors d'oeuvres were tasty and the conversation sprightly. We sat down at the dining room table, so artistically set, and continued our wide-ranged conversation over a delicious meal.

Then, suddenly, it happened. As we nibbled away at our cheesecake and sipped our coffee, the host looked up with his eyes riveted first on mine, then on Anne's, then back at mine. With emphatic, yet puzzled inflection, he articulated the big question, 'Why are so many marriages of people who seem so together and so successful breaking up? We are so shocked when friends of years, with whom we've been together so frequently socially, who seem so happy together, suddenly announce: "It's over".'

I stumbled around for some answers. After all, that's my business, isn't it? Anne tried to answer too. She has also been to seminary, and she is a psychotherapist. We both gave our answers. Frankly, some of them were very good. But ever since that evening in which the conversation suddenly shifted gears, making it one of those never-to-be-forgotten occasions when the six of us got right down to basics, I have been searching my brain, asking questions of others, and asking questions of God. Through prayer and through the searching of Scriptures, I have tried to figure out just why so many marriages that seem so together and successful are breaking up.

I believe that I've come across some answers and also some solutions. These are not final answers, nor are they final solutions. Relationships do not lend themselves easily to once-and-for-all truths that guarantee happiness. At least I am able to share some insights that can challenge you and me to further reflection.

I am convinced many marriages break up because they are built on mythical foundations. What do I mean? There are myths, which are accepted by some of us, that slowly work away on our inner psyche and eventually cause enough damage that our marriages begin to falter.

The Bible is God's Word to you and me. It doesn't tell us everything about God. It doesn't tell us everything about ourselves. It doesn't tell us everything about each other. But the Bible does tell us everything we need to know about how to get along with God, with ourselves, and with each other. The Bible is a textbook of *reality therapy*. It is not a compilation of naive idealisms that paint fantasies that do not square with reality.

The Bible is an earthy book. It has a lot to say about domestic ugliness, marital violence, alcoholism, drug addiction, adultery, dishonesty, ambition, exploitation, manipulation, arrogance and pride. These are only a few of the themes spoken to with great specificity and elaborate illustration.

Not only is ideal marriage described, so is divorce, as we have already seen allowances made for divorce under certain circumstances. However, Jesus reinforces God's initial intention for marriage to be a vehicle that enhances the welfare and the happiness of humankind. He notes the painful disruption that comes – emotionally, physically, and spiritually – when a marriage strays from God's intention and is lived out in a contentious disharmony or one that ends in divorce.

Let's look at a word of advice from the Apostle Paul to his young friend Timothy, who was pastoring the church Paul had founded in Ephesus. Paul has noted in his travels through the Jewish, Greek and Roman world that all people have a weird vulnerability to untruth. We humans are easily deceived by quack remedies and vogue ideologies that come and go at a fairly rapid pace. He urges Timothy to concentrate on the truth that has been revealed to him through the Holy Spirit. He says:

> If you point these things out to the brothers, you will be a
> good minister of Christ Jesus, brought up in the truths of
> the faith and of the good teaching that you have followed.
> Have nothing to do with godless myths and old wives' tales;
> rather, train yourself to be godly (1 Tim. 4:6-7).

Ever since that dinner conversation, as I have been reflecting on this whole matter of marital disharmony and divorce, these words have kept throbbing in my heart and mind: 'Have nothing to do with godless myths and old wives' tales; rather, train yourself to be godly' (1 Tim. 4:7).

The whole attitude of the Apostle Paul, as he shares his concerns with Timothy, is one of nurturing, one of caring, one of counsel, one of advice. It is a gentle, humble word. He wants Timothy to process his instructions in a way that will help him deal healthfully with the believers at Ephesus. He wants him to exhort those for whom he bears pastoral responsibility in a gentle, humble, gracious, counseling mode. He doesn't want Timothy to act in an overbearing, authoritarian manner that puts people down.

How presumptuous it would be of me to stand in the pulpit and pretend personal exemption from the stresses and strains on my own marriage. I dare not bully you into truth. Instead, I must admit that I am a person just as much in process as are you. I must be fed from the Scriptures under the inspiration of the Holy Spirit so as to be able to share with you the discoveries I am making. What I say to you today, as I enter my 60s, hopefully has a depth to it that it would not have had thirty, or even twenty, years ago. And hopefully what I share with you ten years from now will be the result of additional growth. But I do have the responsibility to share with you what is clear and urge you to apply that truth to what may not be as clear.

Paul urges Timothy to avoid 'godless and silly myths'. He is warning him to remain at the center of the faith. How easy it is to be indoctrinated by a society that does not take seriously the truths of God's Word and to wake up to discover we are being destroyed by these godless and silly myths. Instead, we are called to train ourselves in godliness.

I would like to identify several godless and silly myths that can destroy marital harmony and break up your marriage.

Myth one is the *perfect-person* myth.
It goes like this. Boy meets girl. Girl meets boy. And they live happily ever after. This myth says that if you marry the right person you will have a wonderful life together. Your problems will be minimal. Yours will be a storybook love affair.

These kinds of marriages are peopled by handsome men and beautiful women who have darling little children. These people live in lovely homes. They have substantial incomes. They are successful in their work. They are physically agile and enjoy sports. There is plenty of money to do all the things that happily married couples do. Harsh words are never spoken. Disagreements are few and far between. If both are Christians, God will see to it that nothing will happen to this family.

Anne and I married right into this myth. We had an idyllic courtship. It was storybook stuff. There was no question that she was the right person for me and I was the right person for her. People loved to tell the story of how we met in Taiwan and again in Hong Kong, as she was on her way to teach for the summer in Cambodia and I was leading a tour around the world. The story surrounding our meeting in 1963 and wedding in 1964 could provide material for a romantic novel.

But the facts are that Anne and I had problems, and those problems emerged not too long after the honeymoon. The sad thing was that Anne and I lived with the myth for a prolonged period of time, at varying degrees of confusion and frustration, wondering why, since we knew we had married the right person, we were both in pain and causing pain for each other. It took us quite a few years before we were prepared to get the help we needed because we were caught up in the 'perfect-person' myth.

The truth is that every couple is going to have some problems of one kind or another. Our problems will be different from yours. And your problems will differ from those of others, of your friends. Whenever you get two people together, given the many differences and family backgrounds, cultural expectations, and finely tuned differences in individual temperaments, there will be marital difficulties. The sooner you and I discover this truth and put away the myth, the better off our marriages will be.

I'm not saying that God did not want you to marry your spouse. I'm not saying that he or she is not the right person for you. What I'm saying is that there is no such thing as a perfect person, just as there is no such thing as a perfect family. You and I are sinners saved by God's grace. When we marry we still are sinners saved by God's grace, and every couple needs God's grace to survive one day at a time.

I will be the first to admit that Anne and I were quite well-suited for each other in many, many ways. In other ways, we weren't. We've had to learn how to cope with this. I thank God that he brought us together. But the proverbial storybook marriage is actually that – just a story, fictional in nature.

Myth two is the *there's-a-more-perfect-person-out-there* myth. This is a logical extension of the first myth. When you discover that Mr. Perfect isn't so perfect and Mrs. Perfect isn't so perfect, there is a human tendency to wonder if, perhaps, you married the wrong person.

Think back to the circumstances under which you married, if you have been married. I'm speaking now primarily to persons who are married or who have been married, although there are very serious implications for those who are in the process of selecting a mate. The reason I'm reserving this to those of us who are married, or have been married, is that hindsight brings with it an amazingly accurate insight compared to feelings of the present.

Be honest with yourself. Why did you marry that man? What did you think you could get from him? Why did you marry that woman? What did you see in her? What could she give you? Some of us will have to scratch our memories a bit. We are now 10, 20, 30, 40 to 50 years beyond that important decision. You see how culturally conditioned that decision was. He met a role expectation, didn't he? She met a role expectation, didn't she? He looked like he would be so successful. She was so pretty. He was such an athlete. Your mother said he was better for you than the other guy. Your parents said she came from such a good home. Think of all the bartering that goes on in our minds. For some of us, we lived in a time when couples just naturally got married at the time they graduated from high school or from college. So what do they do? Some just married the person they happened to be going with at that point in life. Just think of what it is. Here we are between the age of 18 and 25, seeing the world from that limited perspective, blurred somewhat by that crazy mix of hormones.

So perhaps years later we wake up to the reality that we married a person for the wrong reasons. We can equate that fact with the myth that we, therefore, married the wrong person. Out there, somewhere, is Mr. Perfect or Mrs. Perfect. At the earliest opportunity, we will find that one. In the meantime, let's get rid of this problem character who wasn't right in the first place, who was chosen for some very wrong reasons.

That was what happened to the woman who quite bluntly told her husband of some fifteen years, 'You're a nice guy. I like you a whole lot. You're just not successful enough for me.

You don't make enough money. I'm going to find someone who can provide the lifestyle I deserve.' Don't be shocked. I know a woman who said those exact words to her husband, and I watched her walk away, leaving the one she called 'Mr. Wrong', thinking she had found 'Mr. Right'. Actually, she was not much more aware of what was attracting her to 'Mr. Right' than she was to what had attracted her to her first husband way back then. And how my heart broke as I watched those kids, puzzled expressions on their faces, watching Mommy take off with this new guy. She wanted them to call the new guy Daddy.

And I don't need to reverse the story and talk about men walking off, leaving their wives of many years for a newer and younger model. Sadly, this is all too common.

The truth is that we very well may marry for the wrong reasons. And if given a second chance, we may very well marry again – and maybe even again – for the wrong reasons in a restless search for the perfect person.

And the sad truth is that our society has now begun to endorse this as a valid way of doing business.

Myth three is the *everyone-who-looks-happy-is-happy* myth.

Not everyone who looks happy is happy. You know that. I know that. We know that in general, don't we? It certainly is so easy to be jealous of another couple's apparent, problem-free existence. Isn't it amazing how green the pasture looks on the other side of the fence?

I remember a couple of whom I was jealous. He was handsome and well educated. She was physically gorgeous and seemed to be the perfect mother. They had a beautiful house, cars, and even an airplane. Wherever he went, doors of influence and power were open to him. They took exotic vacations. They were able to charter their own boats and full crew. They were Christians, active in their church and generous with their money. Little did I realize that these two, who looked so happy on the surface, were caged in a relationship of mutual misery. His success was devouring him. He didn't have the time for intimacy. She, hungry for attention, hungry for caring, began to find her solace in that discreetly hidden bottle of wine and that equally discreetly hidden glass that was perpetually filled. She ever so discreetly sipped the wine through the long, lonesome hours day after day, when the kids were at school and her husband was at work.

Little did I know that this couple was so unhappy. What had made her attractive to him made her attractive to other men. The affirmation that she used to get from his compliments about her beauty, she began to find from other men. Ultimately, ever so gradually, she ended up in the arms of another. When he found out, it was over! For as he saw it, she was the bad person. He was the good person. He demonized her, excusing himself, because he had been faithful to her. He wasn't about to go for counsel, and the marriage broke up. For years now, he, having learned the hard way, is scared of commitment and goes from one woman to another, and she from the arms of one man to another.

Those of us who thought they were so happy and wished we had all they had going for us said, 'Isn't that too bad'. And we found another couple to idealize. We settled in, wishing we had all the happiness they have, and will continue to hold them high until something happens to burst our latest fantasy bubble.

The truth is that every married couple has enough problems to break up a marriage if they allow it. Satan would love to get you to throw in the towel. He would love to destroy your marriage by urging you to compare yourself to someone else. The truth is that every couple has their moments of happiness and every couple has their moments of pain. The truth is that no one has it all. The truth is that there is a built-in law of compensation. What looks good and attractive has its flip side of pain-producing potential. How much better it is to work with what we have, however limited that may appear, than to dream about having what someone else seems to have, only to discover that they don't really have it.

Myth four is *the religious* myth.

There are variations to this myth. One is that whether you marry a Christian or not doesn't really make any difference. It will all work out okay. How many young persons get burned in the process of buying into this myth!

We preachers hesitate to speak on this because we don't want to be judgmental. We know what the Bible teaches, that we are not to be 'unequally yoked together with unbelievers'. It seems though to be such a hard teaching. Does it mean that one should never date a non-believer? So we back off at that point, forgetting that seldom does a person marry someone they've not dated. We then try to give the warning to the two who are in love. But then it is too late. The Christian partner kids him or herself into thinking that it really doesn't make any difference. 'I'll lead my partner to faith in Jesus Christ after we get married.' Sometimes that does happen. More often it doesn't. I could give you case history after case history of Christians married to non-believers, some wonderful and some not so wonderful, who yearn for that oneness that could have been theirs in a truly Christian marriage.

Another variation on this religious myth is that all you need to do is to come to Jesus and your problems will disappear. How much blame Jesus has received from people who somehow think that he runs around with a magic wand, instantly healing everything he touches without us respecting certain emotional, spiritual, and physical laws that have direct consequences attached to our breaking of them. Granted, Jesus does – in supernatural ways, on occasion – intervene, bringing miraculous healings to bodies, emotions, and relationships. However, I have discovered in the majority of situations, he works in quiet, gentle, gracious ways, according to the teachings of his Word, making available to us the resources of his power through that sanctifying process of gradual growth toward wholeness in Christ.

The truth is that coming to Jesus isn't going to automatically solve your marital problems. Don't blame him for them. Don't blame him for not taking them away. The truth is that you and I are privileged to appropriate his power to solve those problems over which we have control and to live with those over which we have no control.

Myth five is the *media* myth.

It has some similarities to the 'everyone-who-looks-happy-is-happy' myth. No society in history has been exposed to the extent our society is now exposed to the bombardment of visual stimuli that is so fraudulent. Every society has those who make the same false promises. Every society has had its soft-core pornography that produces its visual fantasies. But none has ever made these quite so readily available in quite such dramatic ways.

Light, camera angles, body building machines, beauty aids, cosmetic surgery, artistic airbrushes, exotic music, virtual reality all can make a mere mortal man look like a god and a mere mortal woman look like a goddess. Body odors disappear. Disease is covered up. Facial problems are glossed over. Emotional breakdowns are hidden. We live in such a fantasy world that we actually believe that the rock stars and movie stars are regular people. We do the same with our so-called 'men of God' and 'women of God'. Watch out if you have too much of a fixation on a particular religious leader. Watch that person closely enough and you will see his or her feet of clay.

Through the media we make superheroes of mere mortals. Then we are crushed when we see our fantasies fall before our eyes. Remember Rock Hudson? We could hardly believe that the before and after pictures were of the same person.

Normally we discard our media creations, forgetting that they all are still alive, when they are no longer useful. Where are the *Playboy* and *Penthouse* centerfolds of the 60s and early 70s now? Most of them are still alive somewhere – middle-aged and experiencing the same effects of Father Time as we all do. They are all still human beings – created in the very image of God. But we made them out to be so much more than human, while at the same time so much less than human, that they are turned into commodities and thrown away when they are no longer useful. Somewhere they sit wondering what happened, why no one calls any more, looking on in broken cynicism as new subjects are made into objects, rocketed into prominence only to be discarded when their usefulness is over.

The truth is that every one of us has our needs. Every one of us battles with weight – too little or too much. Every one of us is either too tall or too short, has too much hair or too little, is too rich or too poor. Every one of us yearns to be accepted by God and by each other. The truth is there is nothing ultimately lonelier than the media myth, as the biography of Marilyn Monroe states so clearly. Madonna will grow old some day. So will Sharon Stone and Gwyneth Paltrow. We all do, don't we?

Myth six is the *incompatibility* myth.
We talked about this in the previous chapter.

Granted, there is alcoholism, child abuse, husband-wife beating, bankruptcy, unfaithfulness, and all those other distortions of relationship to which we have alluded. These are awful things. Granted, there are personalities suffering from pathologies of all sorts which make them, or perhaps us, almost impossible with which to live. So we come to the conclusion that that person no longer deserves us. Or perhaps, that person should have someone better for him or her than us. So we do an end run around the hard work of resolving our differences. We ignore the truth caught up in our myth labeled 'incompatibility'.

As we have already seen, Swiss psychiatrist Paul Tournier did so succinctly underline a great truth when he stated that there is no such thing as incompatibility. Incompatibility is a word that we have created to give us an excuse to get out of a relationship at which we are unwilling to work. So we continue one end run after another, avoiding that privileged fulfillment that comes from working a problem through, a problem that usually involves me just as much as her.

Myth seven is the *hyped-up-romantic-love* myth.

Some couples have sneered at romantic love because of its un-realistic proportions. George Bernard Shaw, in 1908, wrote:

> When two people are under the influence of the most violent, most insane, most delusive, and most transient of passions, they are required to swear that they will remain in that excited, abnormal, and exhausting condition continu-ously until death do them part.

And H. L. Mencken, in 1919, wrote:

> To be in love is merely to be in a state of perceptual anesthe-sia – to mistake an ordinary young man for a Greek god or an ordinary young woman for a goddess!

These two men saw through this hyped-up kind of romantic love. This isn't true love, the biblical understanding of *agape* love, which literally means an act of the will, a choice you and I make to care for, maintain a relationship with and cherish another person. This kind of love you can't fall into– and you can't fall out of. *Agape* is a choice you make that recognizes that mellowing of feeling that sustains us through tough times and ordinary times, not just those times of occasional highs. But, unfortunately, too many of us think there is something wrong if we can't perpetually sustain that high-octane, emotional intensity which one wag says 'involves every part of the body except the brain'.

True love mellows with time and deepens as we increas-ingly become aware that our relationship can be marked by so much more.

Myth eight  is the *low-self-esteem* myth.

Granted, this is a problem for some. I don't deny the importance of us dealing with low self-esteem. Each of us has experienced this to some extent. It is very difficult to think well of yourself.

I will grant that. We all carry self-hate from our childhood into our adult years. We see ourselves as gangly, awkward, fat, skinny, stupid, smart, selfish, arrogant, insensitive or whatever other adjective or verb was used to describe us as a teenager. We carry those pictures into our adult years, failing to integrate into our understanding that it is not really where we are today. But I'm afraid that we can spend the rest of our lives striving for healthy self-esteem in counterbalance to some of those childhood memories in ways that only accentuate that which destroys healthful relationships. We are determined never to be put down again. We are going to fight for our rights. We are going to have that which we earned. 'No husband has the right to whittle away at my self-esteem.' 'No wife has a right to put me down.' 'I'm going to be me! I'm going to assert myself and get what I rightly deserve!'

That's the spirit of our day, isn't it?

But what about the biblical teaching that instructs us to 'count others better than yourself?' How do we deal with those passages that tell us to treat our wives as we would treat our own bodies? How do we handle those passages that, no matter how freed up we become in man-woman roles, do call for wives to be adaptable to their husband's leadership and do call for us to be subject to one another as brothers and sisters in Jesus Christ? The truth is that much of our talk about self-esteem can become an introverted narcissism. It can be an old selfishness revisited with a more acceptable nomenclature.

This myth cries out, 'I have the right to be happy.' The truth is that you do and you don't. You have the right to be joyful. That is true. No other person has been given the right to rob you and me of our joy. But divorce is never the best route to true happiness. It may happen. It may be inevitable. There may be nothing you can do at this point that will restore that breaking or broken marriage. That's why we at St. Andrew's give such attention to our Divorce Recovery Workshop. That is why we're here to minister God's grace and the assurance that there is life after divorce. That is why we are here to do all we can to bring healing and new beginning to those who have suffered and caused suffering that has led to a final severing of vows.

The truth is divorce cannot destroy joy. The truth is that your self-esteem can never ultimately be broken by another human being or ultimately can be found in another human being. Your ultimate self-esteem is made in a right relationship with God in Jesus Christ. The truth is that true happiness is found in him. The reality is that he offers joy to those of us who seek our joy in him.

# CHAPTER 13

WHEN THE HONEYMOON ENDS ...
THE MARRIAGE CAN BEGIN

*Submit to one another out of reverence for Christ*
Ephesians 5:21

There is a whole lot more to marriage than romance.

In fact, romance, as wonderful as it is, can actually mess up a husband-wife relationship. This leads us to the *hyped-up-romantic-love* myth, which has three variations.

Variation one: In order to be happy I have to be married.
Variation two: My marriage partner can make me happy.
Variation three: I have once been deeply in love but now have fallen out of love.

The problem with the first variation is that it is untrue. You don't have to be married to be happy. Somehow, many of us have bought into that fiction. Perhaps we hold to it because marriage was one of our most direct escapes from previous unhappiness. We wanted to get away from home. Or we saw the rest of our friends getting married. They looked so 'happily in love'. We knew we couldn't possibly be happy in our single state.

The fact is that you and I don't have to be married to be happy. An article in the Los Angeles *Times* illustrates how being married is so important to some people. It was published in the early 1990s, during a tough recession in Orange County, California. It reads:

Here is the equation: An already sour California economy plunges further into recession, creating anxiety and longer work hours for those still fortunate enough to be among the ranks of the employed.

Add that to 10,353,000 unmarried residents – 890,000 in Orange County alone. Then multiply it by the AIDS scare.

The result is a booming business for Cupids, who charge between $1,000 and $50,000 to advertise, rifle through files or hunt down prospective mates for singles who believe the elixir to these troubled times is pre-screened conjugal bliss.

'I'm swamped right now,' says Christine O'Keefe, founder of one of the first upscale marriage brokerage businesses in Southern California and the author of *How to Successfully Flirt, Date and Mate!*

'As other people's businesses slow down during this recession, they have more time to think about what's missing in their lives. People I haven't seen in two years are calling to tell me they are at a crossroads, that when things get busy again, they don't want to be trapped without a mate.'

'Quality people are scarce,' says the former manager of the Chicago branch of the Southern California-based video dating service *Great Expectations*. 'If they want to go bimbo-hunting, I send them to the pier.'

I don't think the sentiments expressed in that article are restricted to just times of economic recession. Our economy has recovered. It will have its continuing ups and downs. The fact is that people yearn to be in relationship. They will try all kinds of creative ways to find a partner, a lasting relationship that ultimately leads to marriage.

Frankly, some of the most unhappy people I know are married. Some of the happiest people I know are single. The opposite of both is also true. Marital status should not determine your happiness factor.

The problem with the second variation of this myth is that it, too, is untrue. I think we know that no married partner has the capacity to guarantee our happiness. We know it deep down inside. At the same time, we don't know it. I have that scapegoat mentality that casts around looking for someone who can bear the blame for anything that goes wrong in my life. If I am not happy, it certainly can't be my fault. So I blame my employer, my employees, the governor, the President. Since these people don't buy into my projections of blame, I look closer to home. I am tempted to blame my children, but then that would be a reflection on myself. So why not blame my partner? If she would only be different, more sensitive to my needs, I would be a happier person. When you begin to describe it in these terms you see how untrue this notion is.

The problem with the third variation on this romantic myth is that you simply can't fall out of love. That's a neat idea. It would be quite convenient to blame a marital breakdown on simply having fallen out of love. That is an extremely superficial phrase, used as a rationalization for breaking off vows designed to last a lifetime.

The more I think about it, I am convinced that this romantic myth embodies most of what is wrong with our western understanding of marriage. Some foreign cultures have understood this. Marriages are arranged, often with positive results. I would be the first to protest an arranged marriage. I am much too romantic myself to go along with that concept. I wouldn't want someone else making that important decision for me. However, in my most sober moments, I have a sneaking suspicion that that's basically an ego statement on my part more than a reality-of-marital-happiness statement. I want to shape my own destiny. I don't want anyone else to make those decisions for me.

I prayed and searched for years until I found the one 'perfect' person for me who happened to agree – thinking I was the 'perfect' person for her. She was twenty-three; I was twenty-four. We got married and have been in blissful, romantic love from the moment of the first meeting until now. Do you really believe that? I'm not trying to be cynical about marriage. I'm just trying to be realistic. Even the most complementary couples have their ups and downs. Romance, at its greatest intensity, is difficult to sustain.

We've allowed the romantic myth to carry us away to the point that we have believed our rhetoric. We have convinced ourselves that in order to be happy we have to be married. A partner can make me happy. I guess I have fallen out of love if I no longer feel the way I used to feel about this person for whom I used to have such exotic coronary palpitations.

The fact is that our culture has made so many false promises about romance. Marriage simply can't bear up to that mythical weight. No one person can possibly live up to this kaleidoscope of crazy expectations. Our hormones have a way of going crazy. There is no limit to the number of women I could potentially enjoy. But then I have to ask myself, at what price!

I try to deal with these realities in as honest a way as possible with each couple I marry. We require at least four premarital counseling sessions at St. Andrew's. First, the pastor who will preside at the wedding meets with the couple in an introductory session. There we discuss items noted on a form the couple has filled out in advance. We get to know each other and talk about what Christianity is. If the two are not professing believers in Christ, we encourage them to consider an individual commitment to the Lord as well as to each other.

Then we have two evenings in which the couple meets in a group with other couples who will be married here in the not-too-distant future. There is a lecture session that opens with a description of the various kinds of marriage functioning in our culture. I describe the options of: common law marriage in which two people decide simply to move in with each other without the benefit of a marriage certificate; secular legal marriage by a judge or justice of the peace; religious marriage in which the couple without personal faith chooses to be married by a rabbi, priest, or minister; genuine religious marriage in which both acknowledge their need of God; genuine Christian marriage in which both have repented of sin and put their personal trust in Jesus Christ alone for salvation, making him a part of their marriage; and mixed marriage in which one is a genuine believer marrying another who does not share their faith.

Next I go on to talk about potential problem areas in marriage, some of it involving topics we've discussed in this book. The following session, we give a lecture on the wedding ceremony itself – the vows, some of the distinguishing characteristics of marriages that make it, and they're given the Taylor-Johnson Temperament Analysis Test. The couple answers a battery of questions about themselves and their partner.

Then there is at least one more meeting with the officiating pastor who goes over the results of this emotional profile. They are able to see how they view themselves and how they view each other. Where there are discrepancies, we try to help them recognize their differences and give them ways to minimize them. We want to do everything we can to guarantee that they go into their marriage with their eyes open so as to minimize these discrepancies. We are not trying to destroy romance. We are simply trying to bring as much reality as possible to the relationship.

At the wedding, we read from the Scriptures. We share personal words about marriage and walk the couple through their marriage vows, making comments on the significance of the words that will express their life-long pledge to each other. It is at this time that I find it of enormous significance to distinguish between three kinds of love. For some of us this distinction is old hat. We have heard pastors and counselors talk about it many times. For others, it is a brand-new way of looking at love.

In English we have one word for love. The word is 'love'. I love God. I love my wife. I love my daughters. I love my home, my church, my car, the Angels or the Dodgers, UCLA or USC. I love lightly heated pecan pie topped with vanilla ice cream. You catch what I'm trying to say, don't you? One word in English carries us all the way from the sublime to the ridiculous.

Those who have attended churches most of our lives know that the Greeks in the first century had many words for love. Three in particular are worthy to note.

The first word in Greek is *eros*. Our inclination is to paint this in a negative light. It is the word from which we derive the word 'erotic'. It is a sensual understanding of love. That is not all bad. In fact, we can thank God for this sensual dimension. It is part of his creation. He made us that way. We can use it in ways that exploit others and, in the process, hurt them and ourselves. Or we can take joy that we are people capable of sensual stimulation and that we can, within the bonds of marriage, give and receive such magnificent sexual pleasure. The fact is that we can fall in and out of this erotic magnetism. We are capable of being attracted – before marriage and outside of marriage – in erotic ways that can be quite destructive. *Eros* is a kind of love, but it is not the ultimate love.

The second word is *phileo*, which literally means friendship. It is the stuff of family caring. I will say more about it later.

The third word for love is *agape*. We looked at it briefly in the last chapter. This is the word most frequently used in the New Testament to describe God's love for us and the kind of love God wants us to have for each other. It is a word so carefully defined by the Apostle Paul in 1 Corinthians 13:4-8, when he writes: 'Love is patient, love is kind. It does not envy, it does not boast, it is not proud. It is not rude, it is not self-seeking, it is not easily angered, it keeps no record of wrongs. Love does not delight in evil but rejoices with the truth. It always protects, always trusts, always hopes, always perseveres.' As we've already seen, this kind of love involves an act of the will. Agape is a choice I make. When I love you in this way, I am choosing to stand by you even when I feel that you don't deserve it. Or much more subtly, I feel like I do not deserve it. Marriage is marked by these moments of ambiguity, isn't it?

In the summer of 1985, when Billy Graham held his ten days of meetings at Anaheim Stadium, he told about a time when he and his wife were being interviewed. The reporter asked Dr. and

Mrs. Graham whether they had ever considered divorce. Their immediate mutual response was an emphatic, 'No!' Then Mrs. Graham spoke up somewhat demurely, yet with a degree of firmness in her voice, saying, 'Let me qualify that a bit. Divorce? No! But murder? Sometimes!'

Even the best of relationships will have struggles. One can feel used. One can feel put down. One can feel taken for granted. There will be those moments in which our partner may not actually deserve our love. It is at this moment that love says, 'I choose to care for you. With an act of my will, I will stand by you.'

When we reflect on the nature of our male-female quest for romantic love, it becomes apparent how much more like the *eros* than *agape* is our foundation for marriage. We actually believe that if we find the right person we will experience romantic bliss. When it doesn't turn out that way we are so let down. Some devote their lives to a continuous quest for that ideal romantic partner, only to be disillusioned. These people fall in and out of love. When they fall in love, no one can convince them that they are trying to grasp at something that will prove illusionary. When they fall out of love, no one can convince them that what they are experiencing is a normal feeling and this is the time to begin a healthy marriage – not to terminate the relationship.

I've been so helped in coming to a deeper understanding of our Western, restless quest for romantic love by reading the works of contemporary psychologists. Many of them describe the restless way in which we search for fulfillment outside of ourselves. M. Scott Peck is one of these who writes quite eloquently about the contemporary experience that has been very much a part of his own human odyssey. In his book titled *The Road Less Traveled*, he describes the restless way in which we search for fulfillment outside of ourselves. He describes the frenzied, romantic feelings we have as we pursue that object of our romantic and sexual drive. We are convinced that we are in love. Nothing can stop our hot pursuit of our beloved. The fact is, we are not really in love at all. We are simply having erotic feelings about another person. They fascinate us. We are convinced that if we could only possess that person we could find fulfillment.

Far from being in healthy relationship, we are actually dehumanizing that person, making him or her into an object instead of a subject. It is the same thing we do when we have this desperate 'need' for a new automobile, a new boat, a new house, a new hairstyle, a new set of golf clubs, or new skis. You know what I'm talking about. We convince ourselves that we must redecorate our house. Time seems to stand still as we carry out our quest. We can think of little else until we drive the new car away from the dealership. The fact is, there is going to be a letdown. That automobile will never live up to our expectations. That's why the novelty of a newly decorated home quickly wears off. We begin to see that perhaps we should have picked a different fabric for that chair or a different shade of paint for that wall. Perhaps the money might have been better spent on doing something else.

So we marry that person we 'love' so much. We experience that momentary euphoria. Scott Peck refers to that as a moment of 'cathexis', in which we transcend ourselves. We get outside of ourselves. We think we are sublimely in love, only to fall back into ourselves, seeing the insufficiencies of our partners. Then we conclude, with great regret, that we have fallen out of love.

The fact is no human being can provide that perpetual ecstasy that comes in that initial cathexis. It is at the moment, when the honeymoon is over, that real love can begin. That is when the *agape* is potentially set free. But we must let it be set free.

What we have been calling, to this point, the romantic myth could be renamed the false-god myth. It is the notion that we can find our happiness in someone or something other than in God himself, in Jesus Christ. It just doesn't work out that way. That is not love. That is idolatry. It is as wrong for me to put my wife on a pedestal and worship her as it is for a youngster to put that dreamed-of new bike on a pedestal and worship it, or for an aboriginal tribe person in Papua, New Guinea, to kneel down before that wooden idol and worship it. Augustine was right when he wrote: 'Our hearts are restless until they find their rest in Thee, O God.' There is a God-sized vacuum inside each one of us that cannot be filled by anyone or anything other than Jesus Christ himself. Pascal was right. Western culture is preoccupied with romantic love, only to be let down into a sad disillusionment.

*What then is marriage designed to be?*
It is designed to be a relationship of two different, complementary, growing persons who understand their own limitations and those of their partner and yet are willing to commit to each other and submit to each other as equals till death doth part.

Let's look at three dimensions to this definition I've given for marriage.

One: Marriage is designed to move beyond romance to *relationship.*
It involves companionship. It involves more than two persons who are all too eager to mutually 'rip off' each other. These two are equal, created in the very image of God. They are designed for friendship.

We see this so beautifully articulated for us in Genesis 1:27-28.

> So God created man in his own image, in the image of God he created him; male and female he created them.
> God blessed them and said to them, 'Be fruitful and increase in number; fill the earth and subdue it. Rule over the fish of the sea and the birds of the air and over every living creature that moves on the ground.'

In Genesis 2:18 God says, 'It is not good for the man to be alone. I will make a helper suitable for him.' Isn't that a marvelous picture? Every one of us needs a friend. One of the best kinds of friends is a member of the opposite sex. No, that is not the only kind of friendship. Your husband or your wife isn't to be your only friend. However, your husband or your wife can be your best friend. In some marriages, this happens naturally. For the majority of us, it takes work.

I remember back in the late 1960s and through the 1970s, when so many couples began to live together without the benefit of marriage. These were persons who had never been married before. It wasn't that they had been burned by a bad experience. What they would tell me was that they had seen friends who, prior to getting married, had such a wonderful friendship, only to have that friendship destroyed by a 'piece of paper', the marriage certificate. They observed parents who had allowed the attrition of years to destroy companionship, relationship, and friendship. These young idealists were determined not to let the institution of marriage destroy something good they had going.

Why are there so many marriages of people, who seem to have so much going for them, breaking up? One answer is that they have lost sight of the friendship factor. Each of us needs companionship. When we neglect friendship with our partner we are so much more vulnerable to another legitimate friendship becoming distorted into something that detracts from our marriage – often an affair. Ironically, often the 'new love' isn't necessarily more beautiful or smarter or wealthier. It's just that 'he understands me' or that 'she listens to me, and we're such good friends.'

Just what is the stuff of friendship? It is an honest understanding of my insecurities and my willingness to share them with someone else who's willing to listen and share their insecurities with me. Friendship is knowing that I can be honest and be accepted in my weakness. That's what marriage is intended to be: two people in relationship; two people who are companions; two people who are not identical but are complementary; two people who are friends. Instead, we are dulled to each other's needs. We become defensive. We become lonely. Our eyes restlessly look away to find someone else who will meet our needs. When my wandering eyes cruise the scene, her eyes watch me. I turn back to her momentarily, hoping that maybe a flicker of companionship and friendship and intimacy that was once there will revive itself. She quickly turns, cruises the scene, looking for someone with whom she will not have to be so defensive because he is not so defensive. So I zig, and she zags. When she zigs, I zag. And the relationship breaks down just a little more each time.

Unfortunately, too many examples of this come readily to mind.

I remember one couple who had just about everything going for them for which two people could ask. She was beautiful. He was handsome. Both had fine educations. They had two darling children. She had her business. He had his. They were fun to be with as a couple. They seemed so compatible. But instead of celebrating each other's successes, they devolved into a subtle competition. Instead of enjoying a healthy friendship, they began to spar with each other. The zigging and the zagging began. At first, she resented his preoccupation with work. She expressed her complaint. He began to modify his behavior. At about the same time, she became preoccupied with her work. And he complained about her emotional inaccessibility. They both wanted more – more money, more adult toys, more travel. Their educational goals for their children heightened. Their daughter developed an eating disorder. They couldn't accept that they might be part of her problem. Each would complain to me as to how the other was not meeting their needs. He became more and more consumed with his work, unable to see that he was cutting off the very intimacy with her for which he craved. She too worked harder, while gradually developing a deepening friendship with another man who gave her the attention, bought her the gifts, and provided the romance for which she craved. At first she rationalized around the fact that he was married. Then her husband found out. His hurt turned to anger. You know the rest of the story. You too have seen it so often. She left him for the other man who, by this time, had filed for divorce. The kids were confused. Their antisocial behavior intensified. My heart broke as I watched two of my dear friends go their separate ways in bitterness and deep hurt. How did the story end? It hasn't yet. They both drifted into second marriages. Years went by. The man she married proved to be as unfaithful to her as he was to his first wife. Her heart was broken. And he could never quite please his second wife. She finally left him for an old high school sweetheart. He seems so lonely and so adrift. The kids are grown up now and replicating the same kind of behavior.

I am stubborn enough to believe that this all didn't have to happen. I love these two people. They could have had a marriage as it was designed to be. They somehow never quite moved beyond romance to relationship. They expected so much from each other. I am convinced their expectations let them down. They hungered for more – when that more was potentially right there, if they could have only seen it.

Two: *Marriage is designed for growth.*
How easy it is to forget that life is not intended to be static. It is dynamic. We are intended to be growing persons. This is so beautifully illustrated by the life of Jesus Christ. Who came into this world with more going for him than Jesus? Yet, the first thirty years of his life are capsuled in one verse which reads, 'And Jesus grew in wisdom and stature, and in favor with God and men' (Luke 2:52). The word here 'grew' means 'increased'. It implies a continuing, present action. This action has an intellectual, a physical, a spiritual, and a social dimension to it.

So we have a husband and we have a wife. They come together in marriage. At that moment, when they take the vows, they have certain presuppositions about each other. They're inclined to believe that they will always think, feel, and act the way they do in the present. In some ways, that is true. In other ways, it isn't. The fact is that each of them is going to grow at different speeds.

For example, before I got married, I had spent 24 years of my life in one set of intellectual, physical, spiritual, and social growth patterns. Anne had spent 23 years of her life in one set of intellectual, physical, spiritual, and social growth patterns that were unique to her. I knew what I expected of her. She knew what she expected of me. We both thought that we were perfect for each other.

It is amazing how perfectly we met those expectations until the honeymoon was over. Then she picked up her normal growth pattern, and I picked up mine. I had my defensiveness. She had hers. I would mention my expectations of her. She would mention her expectations of me. She couldn't figure out why I wasn't more domestic like her father who loved to spend weekends around the house – barbecuing, creating exotic salad combinations, and watching football, basketball, or baseball on TV. I couldn't figure out why she wasn't interested in attending some of my seminary classes with me. She couldn't figure out why I needed less sleep than she needed. I couldn't figure out why she wasn't more excited about going to New York every weekend to work at the Fifth Avenue Presbyterian Church alongside me, after she had taught five days and then had done the household tasks on Saturday.

So the years went by. The children came along. Anne plowed her energy into mothering. I plowed my energy into what, on the one hand, might be perceived as pastoring the churches to which I was called while, on the other hand, might be viewed as building my own career. I could hide behind the sacred calling of ministry, and she could hide behind the sacred calling of motherhood. Five years went by; ten years went by, plus a few. By now we were both in our late thirties. An ever-so-imperceptible shift began to happen. Wherein I had been so caught up in my career and Anne had been so caught up in nurturing, we both had slowed down our frenetic pace in each of these pursuits. Unknown to each other, we were wistfully looking at the other. I saw her in the fulfillment she was having in nurturing, and I saw the dead end of an achievement-oriented life. Little did I realize that she was looking wistfully at me, realizing we wouldn't have the girls with us forever, nurturing couldn't go on unstopped. She saw the strokes I was getting out there in my achievements. It was like we crossed like ships in the night, my moving toward her orientation and her moving toward mine. Strange, isn't it?

Fortunately, we both were readers. We did our reading separately. I guess we were fearful to share the realities of what we were discovering. I read a book titled *Transformations* by UCLA psychiatrist Roger L. Gould. Gould described how so subtly our orientations can shift. He described adult developmental patterns. He wrote about the demons of childhood and the myths that we carry into adult life. He described how men tend to spend their twenties and thirties in achievement orientation, trying to accomplish more and more in their work. He noted how women, at that time in American life, tended to emphasize their more nurturing qualities during their twenties and thirties. Then, almost imperceptibly, the two orientations shift. The man looks at his wife and sees the fulfillment she derives from nurturing, and he wants more of that. She looks at him and sees the fulfillment he appears to receive from his accomplishments professionally, and she wants some of that. I was so impressed by what I was reading. This sounded so much like Anne's and my relationship. He was describing our life, our odyssey.

One night I came home and saw that Anne had bought a copy of the same book. By now she was going to seminary. I hadn't been able to figure out why this woman, who didn't want to go to class with me when I was in seminary, was now preoccupied with theology. We began to compare notes. We both read *Men in Mid-Life Crisis* by Jim Conway. I read *Seasons of a Man's Life* by Daniel J. Levinson of Yale University.

Things were happening inside her. We were becoming different. She was growing faster than I was growing, just like years before when I was growing faster than she was growing. I was experiencing what I have come to know as 'development envy'. I had to deal with some anger. Look what she was accomplishing; look what she was experiencing; look how she was growing while I was busy trying to do my job and paying the bills, even to the point of having to take an occasional vacation alone.

Fortunately, there was help available. The help of the reading we were doing. The help of those occasional conversations when we both let the defenses down long enough to acknowledge what was going on inside each of us. There was the help of therapy from professional counselors who could guide the process, assuring us that growth was okay and that we dare not manipulate each other's growth. And there was the help of friendship, people who simply loved us and were willing to stand by us.

This developmental growth process, at times, functioned somewhat smoothly. At other times, it was a wrenching, awkward, threatening experience. And I must be honest to acknowledge that the nineteen-month, life-and-death struggle of our young adult daughter, Suzanne, with Hodgkin's Disease, and the subsequent, torturing grief process since her death in September of 1991, had a way of adding a horrendous, complicating dynamic to this developmental process.

The exciting fact is that we are learning to understand each other's growth and to communicate with each other about that growth. We are increasingly able to celebrate the uniqueness that we both bring as growing persons to our marriage. This growth dynamic continues as we move toward our fourth decade of marriage.

Three: *Marriage is designed for mutual submission.*
Ephesians 5:21-33 is one of the most-often quoted passages about marriage in the Bible. Our perspective about how we view marriage is so determined by how we read these verses. Also, how we read these verses is very much determined by the perspective we bring to them.

It is so easy to play games with Ephesians 5:22-23, which reads, 'Wives, submit to your husbands as to the Lord. For the husband is the head of the wife as Christ is the head of the church, his body, of which he is the Savior.' That is pretty heavy stuff for a male chauvinist, isn't it? How many a defensive male, harassed by his own frustrations and failures at being a Christian husband, pulls out those verses at the most opportune moments and whips his wife with them. They are natural, when quoted out of context, to support the selfish interest of the male.

How many a wife, when hassled by life and her own failures and frustrations, meets his coercive onslaught with this manipulative quote from Ephesians 5:28-29: 'In the same way, husbands ought to love their wives as their own bodies. He who loves his wife loves himself. After all, no one ever hated his own body, but he feeds and cares for it, just as Christ does the church....' Though she may not actually quote these words as he quotes his favorite verses to her, she thinks about them. How naturally, when quoted out of context, they support the natural selfish interest of the female.

Luxuriate in turning these around. Men, let's remind ourselves of the tenderness and care and love that we need to show our wives. Women, don't forget your responsibility to adapt yourself to your husband, respecting his leadership.

All of us, let's not forget Ephesians 5:21, one of the most neglected verses out of this passage, which reads, 'Submit to one another out of reverence for Christ'. This verse combines the rest of the biblical teaching, helping our eyes to meet as equals, viewing each other as precious, being willing to submit ourselves to each other as brothers and sisters in Jesus Christ. Mutual submission!

When Anne and I remember and practice mutual submission, our clever game playing goes out the window. We become very special, sensitive, caring persons to each other, loving companions, willing to make sacrifices so as to guarantee each other's growth.

Don't let what I've shared with you weigh you down with guilt. Remember, we are all in this together. The apex of the Christian faith is not having your act together. The high point of our faith is to humbly receive the grace and forgiveness of Jesus Christ as we lay our burden down at the foot of the cross. Every one of us, no matter what stage we are at, has the need for his daily forgiveness. He desires to set you free, guiding you by his Holy Spirit as one always in process through the good times and the bad times and in the in-between times!

I am afraid that some of us never learn the elusive yet simple truths. The idea of mutual submission is so alien to the modern spirit. We bought in to the crazy fantasy, the perpetual honeymoon. Then we are disappointed when no relationship lives up to that expectation. You and I have the privilege of discovering those amazing truths reflective of those paradoxes taught by Jesus. The first shall be last. The last shall be first. The person who finds himself putting self first in a marriage will lose himself and the marriage. The person who loses oneself in mutual submission to one's spouse will ultimately find oneself, discovering that when the honeymoon ends ... the marriage can begin. It's then and only then that you and I can have the family we want!

# GENERAL INDEX

# Don't they make a Lovely Couple?

*Six important Questions you need to Face about your Marriage*

## Ann and John Benton

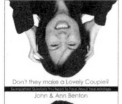

Six important Questions you need to Face about your Marriage

Only half of today's marriages stick – why is that?

The social revolution has made marriage fairer and unacceptable behaviour more 'frowned upon' so shouldn't our marriages be healthier and more long-lasting?

Why is it that an institution that forms the basis of society is in crisis? And what can we do to improve things?

Here are 6 questions to ask yourselves if you are preparing for, or are already part of, a marriage. This book won't make you feel guilty and suggest impossible solutions (we've all read THOSE sort of books before!). It'll make you realise what you can do and suggest a plan to implement it.

Is your marriage important? – Show that it is!

John and Ann Benton have developed and run practical Marriage orienting and enrichment seminars to the benefit of numerous couples (and couples to be). John is a church minister, author and magazine editor,

ISBN 1-84550-046-6

# Aren't they lovely when they're asleep?

*Lessons on unsentimental parenting*

## Ann Benton

Ann Benton used to run parenting skills classes in local schools. People kept saying "This is great, where do you get this stuff?" She came clean "Actually, it's from the Bible."

This book contains the wisdom distilled from Ann's popular seminars on parenting the next generation. She uses a 'God's eye view' of what we are really like in order to help people who are seeking to be responsible parents in an increasingly child-centred society.

You will learn six key concepts: accept, beware, communicate, discipline, evaluate and fear the Lord. These are applied with understanding and sensitivity.

Each short, punchy chapter is rounded off with thought-provoking questions that will make you want to wake them up and try some new ideas!

*'A welcome and stimulating addition to contemporary literature on parenting. Ann's book helps parents to take the long view of parenting - What are we doing? We are growing adults!'*

**Sheila M. Stephen,
counsellor and teacher on parenting skills**

*Ann Benton brings a wealth of Biblical wisdom, as well as a great deal of sound common sense to this subject. Over the past years I have learned a great deal from Ann's seminars on parenting, and also from her example as a mother. I am delighted that she has written this book, and would commend it warmly, especially to new parents.*

**Sharon James, author and conference spe**

ISBN 1-85792-876-8

# Christian Focus Publications

publishes books for all ages
Our mission statement –

STAYING FAITHFUL

In dependence upon God we seek to help make His infallible
Word, the Bible, relevant. Our aim is to ensure that the Lord
Jesus Christ is presented as the only hope to obtain forgive-
ness of sin, live a useful life and look forward to heaven with
Him.

REACHING OUT

Christ's last command requires us to reach out to our world
with His gospel. We seek to help fulfill that by publishing
books that point people towards Jesus and help them develop
a Christ-like maturity. We aim to equip all levels of readers for
life, work, ministry and mission.

Books in our adult range are published in three imprints.
*Christian Focus* contains popular works including biographies, commentaries, basic doctrine and Christian living.
Our children's books are also published in this imprint.
*Mentor* focuses on books written at a level suitable for Bible College and seminary students, pastors, and other serious readers. The imprint includes commentaries, doctrinal
studies, examination of current issues and church history.
*Christian Heritage* contains classic writings from the past.

Christian Focus Publications, Ltd
Geanies House, Fearn,
⌐ire, IV20 1TW, Scotland, United Kingdom
info@christianfocus.com

of our titles visit us on our website
www.christianfocus.com